THE TARNS OF LAKELAND
VOL.2: EAST

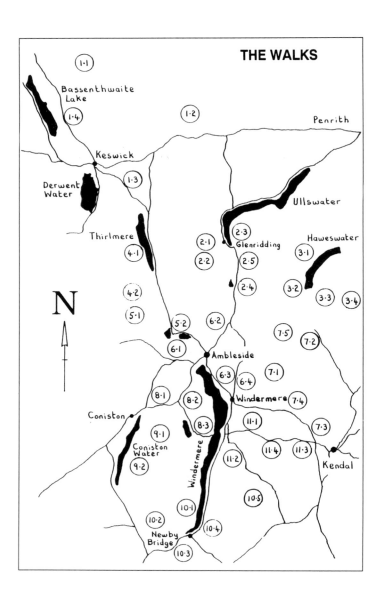

THE WALKS

THE TARNS OF LAKELAND
VOL.2: EAST

by

John and Anne Nuttall

Maps and drawings by
John Nuttall

CICERONE PRESS
MILNTHORPE, CUMBRIA

© John and Anne Nuttall 1996
ISBN 1 85284 210 5
A catalogue record for this book is available from the British Library.

ACKNOWLEDGEMENTS
Our thanks go to Lorna Jones of Cumbria Tourist Board
and to Bob McMillan of Limefitt Park for their help during
the preparation of this book.

ADVICE TO READERS

Readers are advised that whilst every effort is taken by the authors to ensure the accuracy of this guidebook, changes can occur which may affect the contents. A book of this nature with detailed descriptions and detailed maps is more prone to change than a more general guide. New fences and stiles appear, waymarking alters, there may be new buildings or eradication of old buildings. It is advisable to check locally on transport, accommodation, shops etc. Even rights of way can be altered, paths can be eradicated by landslip, forest clearances or changes of ownership. The publisher would welcome notes of any such changes.

Other books by the same authors:

The Tarns of Lakeland Vol 1: West
The Mountains of England and Wales Vol1: Wales
The Mountains of England and Wales Vol2: England
Walking round The Lakes
Weekend Walks in the Peak District

CONTENTS

INTRODUCTION 7
NOTES 9

CHAPTER 1   NORTHERN TARNS
Walk 1.1   Over Water and the Uldale Fells 13
Walk 1.2   Scales Tarn and Bowscale Fell 18
Walk 1.3   Tewet Tarn and High Rigg 25
Walk 1.4   Carlside Tarn 30

CHAPTER 2   PATTERDALE TARNS
Walk 2.1   Red Tarn and Brown Cove 36
Walk 2.2   Hard Tarn and Nethermost Pike 42
Walk 2.3   Place Fell 50
Walk 2.4   Caudale Moor and Brothers Water 56
Walk 2.5   Hayeswater, Brock Crags and Angle Tarn 61

CHAPTER 3   HAWESWATER TARNS
Walk 3.1   High Raise to Bampton Common 68
Walk 3.2   High Street 75
Walk 3.3   Branstree and Swindale 80
Walk 3.4   Wet Sleddale 86

CHAPTER 4   WYTHBURN TARNS
Walk 4.1   Harrop Tarn to Launchy Tarn 91
Walk 4.2   Steel Fell and Greenup Edge 96

CHAPTER 5   GRASMERE TARNS
Walk 5.1   Sergeant Man and Easedale Tarn 102
Walk 5.2   Alcock Tarn 109

CHAPTER 6   AMBLESIDE TARNS
Walk 6.1   Loughrigg Fell 115
Walk 6.2   Scandale Tarn and Red Screes 120
Walk 6.3   Middlerigg Tarn 127
Walk 6.4   Dubbs Reservoir to Holehird 130

CHAPTER 7   KENTMERE AND LONGSLEDDALE TARNS
   Walk 7.1   Kentmere Tarn 137
   Walk 7.2   Skeggles Water 140
   Walk 7.3   Potter Fell 144
   Walk 7.4   Kemp Tarn 151
   Walk 7.5   Yoke to Kentmere Reservoir 153

CHAPTER 8   HAWKSHEAD TARNS
   Walk 8.1   Tarn Hows 162
   Walk 8.2   High Wray and Blelham Tarn 167
   Walk 8.3   Claife Heights 174

CHAPTER 9   GRIZEDALE FOREST TARNS
   Walk 9.1   Grizedale Forest 180
   Walk 9.2   Satterthwaite to Arnsbarrow Tarn 186

CHAPTER 10   SOUTHERN TARNS
   Walk 10.1   High Dam 190
   Walk 10.2   Hay Bridge 193
   Walk 10.3   Bigland Tarn and Canny Hill 197
   Walk 10.4   Cartmel Fell 204
   Walk 10.5   Whitbarrow 210

CHAPTER 11   SOUTH-EASTERN TARNS
   Walk 11.1   Bowness 216
   Walk 11.2   Winster Vale 220
   Walk 11.3   Rather Heath and Cunswick Scar 226
   Walk 11.4   Atkinson Tarn 232

ALPHABETICAL LIST OF THE EASTERN TARNS 236

INTRODUCTION

We were sitting in a small cafe at Waterhead and it was raining. The rain was coming down in a determined sort of way, and it wasn't going to stop. But we had planned a week tarn hunting among the Eastern Fells and it was time to start. So with heavy sacks laden with tent, sleeping bags and supplies for several days we turned our backs on the lake and headed east. Walking in the rain is always better than it seems looking out of the window, and it was good to be at last on the way. As we crossed the hillside little becks splashed silver over the rocks, the trees and fields smelt fresh and new, while all about us were the flowers. By the time we got to Kentmere we had counted ninety different species, the rain had stopped, and as we emerged onto the open fell the clouds parted. In the warmth of the evening sunshine we chose a spot by the beck and set up our tent under a blue sky mirrored in the surface of a tarn.

That was the first of the expeditions to the Eastern Fells, and there have been many others, as tarns were visited and revisited and walks planned to include them all. Sometimes we stayed at farms and cottages, while other nights throughout the year were spent in our small tent high among the fells. On spring mornings we have woken to the song of the lark, a tiny speck high in the sky, and the insistent call of new-born lambs. The long days of summer have seen lazy afternoons beside a tarn, but most memorable are winter camps, with the mountains brilliant white and the tarns frozen and still, while from camps spent on the summits the colours of sunset and dawn are unsurpassed.

Tarn hunting is full of delights and surprises, and the biggest surprise of all is when a tarn has vanished. We had come a long way to visit Scalebarrow Tarn, and had already spent a long time looking. On the almost flat expanse of fell there was grass, a few rocks, a few sheep, and nothing else. The tarn was marked clearly on the map. Heaton Cooper had found it. But we couldn't. It was a perfectly clear day, and we could see for miles, but of Scalebarrow Tarn there was not a sign. We must be in the wrong place, we told ourselves, and began to take bearings on the surroundings, but careful measurements only confirmed our position. We were standing exactly in the middle of the tarn, and it didn't exist.

But missing tarns were unusual. Far more often the surprises were the discoveries. Tiny flecks of blue, hardly noticeable on the map without a magnifying glass, would sometimes prove to be no more than shallow peaty pools, but others were unnamed gems. There was no way of telling in advance, we just had to go and look.

There was the vanished Podnet Tarn, mysteriously omitted by the Ordnance Survey and then restored. There was Launchy Tarn, where we were watched by shy deer on the fells above Thirlmere. Among the transitory pools of High Rigg was a lovely tarn with an island golden with lesser spearwort, while hidden on the very edge of the crags overlooking Kentmere we found Rainsborrow Tarn. No path led to it, there were no cairns, and it had even escaped the notice of Wainwright.

It is fashionable these days to say that Lakeland is crowded, and at the height of summer some of the popular routes are indeed busy, yet so few people turn aside from the path that within yards the fellside is deserted. Tucked out of sight on the climb from Far Easedale to High Raise we found Ash Crags Tarn, another secret tarn lay on the lip of the fells above Mosedale, while among the tiniest was one of the best, Satura Crag Tarn, a shy rocky pool perched on the edge of the fell high above Hayeswater.

With eyes fixed on the high fells, the countryside around Windermere had been left until last, but here too were unexpected delights. The white cliffs of Whitbarrow and Cunswick Scar are made of limestone, a paradise of flowers. In Grizedale Forest dragonflies hovered over the tarns, and red squirrels were a flash of colour among the branches, while the quiet lanes and fields of the Winster Valley seemed little changed since the days of Wordsworth.

It was late in the afternoon as we reached the tall stone column of Thornthwaite Beacon, and already below us the valleys were deep in shadow. But summer evenings on the tops are long, and out of a clear blue sky the sun still shone as we set up the tent beside the stone wall. There was hardly a breath of wind, and the view was sharp and clear right across Lakeland. Everyone had gone down long ago, and save the sheep nothing moved in the wide sweep of the Kentmere Fells and the long ridge of High Street. Slowly long shadows stretched out across the fell until, as the sun dipped towards the distant blue-grey fells, the air grew chill and we sat in the tent doorway with our sleeping bags pulled up around us. Gradually the light grew orange, and the sky a deeper blue until at last a thin line of cloud on the horizon swallowed the disc of the sun. Overhead one by one the stars were coming out.

It was the final expedition. We had reached the end of a long journey, for after nearly four years spent visiting the tarns our explorations were complete. And how many are there in the Lake District? We make it 335, but even a lifetime is too short to know every corner of Lakeland, and round the next rock may yet be an undiscovered tarn. The exact number is not important, for the fun of tarn hunting is the joy of walking in the Lake District, and someone who is tired of the Lakes is tired of life.

NOTES

Selection of the Tarns

"Baysbrown Tarn is not a tarn" said the owner when we asked his permission for a visit, "It is a duck pond". A tarn, says our dictionary, is a small mountain lake and the word comes from the Old Norse word *tjorn*. The Freshwater Biological Association, taking a more scientific approach, defines it as one in which the chief plant is the bottle sedge, whereas in a lake it is the common reed. Yet science comes a long way behind Wordsworth's description of Blea Tarn, "A liquid pool that glittered in the sun". But what exactly is a tarn? How were we to select from the innumerable patches of blue scattered across the map?

There were plenty of suggested rules: A tarn should be natural, it should have a permanent outflow, not dry up in the summer; it shouldn't be too shallow and it should have a name. Well, if tarns had to meet all those stringent qualifications, then many of the loveliest tarns in the Lake District would be eliminated. Tarn Hows isn't natural, Blind Tarn hasn't got an outflow, Snipeshow Tarn dries up, and Foxes Tarn is only a few inches deep, and while some tarns have three or more names, others have none at all.

It is impossible to be precise about it and any selection is bound to be a personal one, for when seen in sparkling sunlight under a blue sky even the merest puddle can look enchanting. In the end we have included all the tarns named on the Ordnance Survey maps which come within the boundary of the Lake District National Park. To these we have added all those commonly accepted as tarns, though not named on the maps, and finally we have included those which because of their size or situation could not be ignored.

Area Covered

All the tarns described in these two volumes lie within the boundary of the Lake District National Park. Volume 1 covers all the tarns of Western Lakeland and Volume 2 covers the Eastern Lakes. The dividing line runs through Bassenthwaite Lake, over High Seat, High Raise and Silver How to Skelwith Bridge, and finally along the A593 and down through Coniston Water.

The Walks

There are 40 walks in Volume 2 and each has been devised to visit one or more tarns. The position of the walks is given on the map on page 2. Some named tarns are not visited on the walks because either they have disappeared, or are now overgrown and not worth visiting. They are, however, included in the alphabetical list at the end of the book. Similarly some tarns are private and there is no public access. These too have been included in the alphabetical list. Many reservoirs, although artificial, are now regarded as tarns, and these too have been included in the alphabetical list.

Access

There is a fine tradition of open access to most of the high fells of the Lake District and all the routes described either follow rights of way or routes that are in common use by hill-walkers. We have completed all the walks without problems, but the fact remains that there is no universal right of access to the hills.

Maps

The detailed route maps are at a scale of 1:25,000. Wherever possible they have been drawn with north at the top which is how most people like them, but in a few cases this rule has been broken in order to avoid splitting a map awkwardly over two pages. A key to the maps is given on page 11.

Ordnance Survey maps are generally reckoned to be the best in the world and no-one will be disappointed with an investment in them. A good overall picture of the Lake District is given by the 'one-inch' Lake District map. The walks are also covered at a slightly larger scale by the more modern 1:50,000, Landranger Series sheets 90, 96 and 97.

However the best maps of all are the 1:25,000 Outdoor Leisure maps The English Lakes. The majority of the tarns in this volume are covered by the four sheets of this series, except the extreme north of the National Park which appears on Pathfinder 576, and the far south, on Pathfinder 626 and 627.

Equipment

The walks in this book range from the easiest afternoon stroll to energetic expeditions over the highest mountains. The weather, however, can turn even a simple walk into an adventure. For all the walks, boots, waterproof and windproof clothing are advisable, while for the high fells a compass and an ability to use it are essential.

In winter conditions the Lake District mountains can be arctic and many of the routes described are then only suitable for very experienced fell-walkers.

Weather Reports

The weather in the Lake District, as in all mountainous areas, can change remarkably rapidly. The weather reports given on television and radio are at best a rough guide and apply to valley conditions only. If you are going high on the fells a much better and detailed weather report, including fell top conditions, is available on: Windermere (01768) 775757. Many shops and Information Centres also display copies of this report.

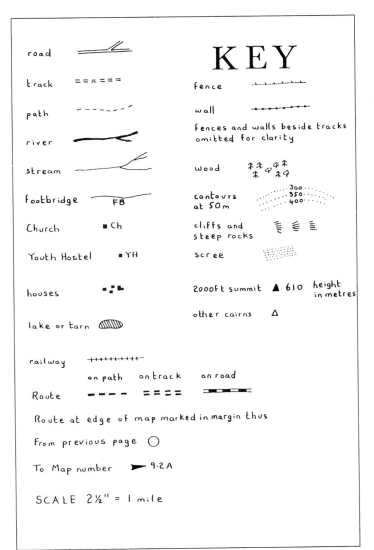

KEY

road

track `= = = = =`

path `- - - - -`

river

stream

footbridge FB

Church ■ Ch

Youth Hostel ■ YH

houses

lake or tarn

railway `+++++++++++`

fence `------/-/-/-`

wall `•••••••••`

Fences and walls beside tracks
omitted for clarity

wood

contours
at 50m

300
350
400

cliffs and
steep rocks

scree

2000ft summit ▲ 610 height
in metres

other cairns △

Route

on path on track on road

`- - - -` `= = = =`

Route at edge of map marked in margin thus

From previous page ◯

To Map number ► 9.2 A

SCALE 2½" = 1 mile

Jed

1: Northern Tarns

WALK 1.1: OVER WATER AND THE ULDALE FELLS

Tarns:	Over Water
	Chapelhouse Reservoir
	Little Tarn (Nevin Tarn)
Distance:	6½ miles
Ascent:	850ft
Summary:	Easy walking skirting the deserted Uldale Fells, then quiet field paths lead back to Over Water.
Starting Point:	(GR 250352) Over Water, 1 mile south of Uldale. Ample parking by the road side.

In a hollow among the northern fells, far beyond Skiddaw and almost out of the Lake District, lies a trio of quiet tarns. Over Water, since its enlargement in the 1920s to supply Wigton with water, is the fourth largest in the Lakes, but tucked away out of sight and reached only by narrow lanes that amble through tiny hamlets and past isolated farmhouses, this is a tranquil and peaceful area.

To the east rise the Uldale Fells, domed heathery and grassy summits where the sheep are no longer troubled by wolves, for Uldale means Wolf's Dale, while to the west is the isolated upthrust of Binsey. The steep conical shape and rocky slopes of this little hill remind one of the rugged mountains which make up the core of central Lakeland; and the similarity is no coincidence for the rock is Borrowdale Volcanic, a long narrow band which wraps round the northern flank of the Skiddaw Range.

Little Tarn, the smallest of the three and also the highest, feeds a beck which trickles down to Over Water and the outflow continues towards Chapel House to merge with the River Ellen. Rising on the Uldale Fells, just below the glacial gap known as Trusmadoor, the river passes through Chapelhouse Reservoir and then meanders westwards for 20 miles until it reaches the sea at Maryport. Like Ravenglass far to the south, Maryport was a Roman harbour, built originally for an invasion of Ireland that never came, but it wasn't until the eighteenth century that the town was developed. Once called Ellenfoot it was renamed in honour of Mary, the wife of Humphrey Senhouse who expanded the port to serve the coal trade of north-western Cumbria.

It was April when last we visited Over Water. Fleeting glimpses of the sun peeped from between ragged clouds as we wandered across fields full of new-born lambs and down lanes covered in primroses, and looking across

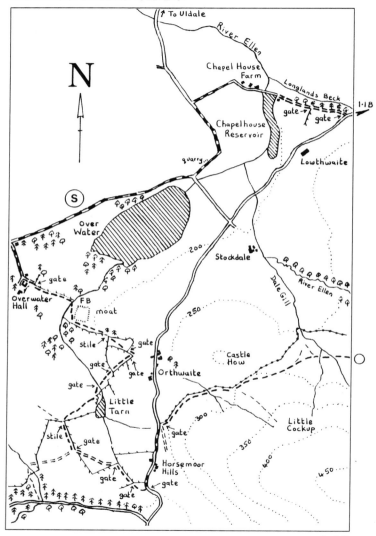

1.1A

the tarn to the distant mass of Skiddaw it seemed as if we had left Lakeland behind. But as we reached the road where the houses cluster together in the hamlet of Longlands, and turned off to walk beside the beck across the short cropped turf, the open fellside came as a surprise; suddenly we had stepped back over the edge and once again were among the hills.

ROUTE DESCRIPTION

Over Water (*Orri's lake or the lake of the black grouse*)
Heading east along the wide-verged road past Waterside Wood, the grassy Uldale Fells form a fine background to Over Water. This privately owned lake with its fringe of trees is rarely used these days by the waterboard, and now blends naturally into the scene.

Chapelhouse Reservoir
Forking left at the junction towards Uldale and Ireby the road leads uphill past a small disused quarry and over the brow of the hill, where you turn right down the lane to Chapel House Farm. Just past the farm the track crosses the foot of the long, narrow, and rather gloomy Chapelhouse Reservoir, which is owned by North West Water and supplies Wigton, then keeping to the right above Longlands Beck, the track climbs by the fence to join the road.

Uldale Fells (*Wolves' valley hills*)
A few yards towards Longlands, and after crossing the beck, go over a ladder stile by a gate and follow the track beside the wall. The beck hides shyly out of sight, while to the left rises Longlands Fell whose slopes contrast with the limed and fertile fields of the valley floor. Passing the spoil from the Longlands Copper Mine, a mid-nineteenth-century trial level which has been adapted since as a water supply, the path swings on round the hillside above the spectacular hidden ravine of the River Ellen.

The river is crossed by a sheepfold, and ahead is the striking gash of Trusmadoor, a glacial melt-water channel, but our route turns right beside the stream before climbing a groove in the hillside. The path then contours along the slopes of Great Cockup, which contrary to expectations is named after a game bird, the woodcock. To the north-west Over Water can be seen in the valley beneath the rounded bulk of Binsey, and this fell, the most northerly described in Wainwright's seven volumes, was reputedly the last in Lakeland to be enclosed by walls.

After crossing two tributaries of Dale Gill the path follows the wall past Castle How, possibly a fortified site in the Dark Ages, and rounding the bump of Little Cockup, Bassenthwaite Lake comes into view. Crossing another stream the path drops to a farm track which leads out to a lane where you turn left.

Over Water

Little Tarn

The lane descends gently past Horsemoor Hills Farm and at the head of the valley to the left the white streak of Dash Falls can be seen. At the bend take the track, which is a public footpath, uphill through a series of stiles and gates until, nearly at the top, a signpost points right along the hedge. This is a good spot from which to admire the Skiddaw Fells and the vast expanse of the more remote Uldale Fells.

At the end of the hedgerow, the path leads over a ladder stile down towards Orthwaite, descending through gorse bushes to the corner of Little Tarn with its screen of birch and willow. Set in a hollow in the farmland the tarn is surrounded by a fence and there is no access to the water's edge.

Overwater Hall

Crossing a gated bridge the waymarked path leads across the fields, then

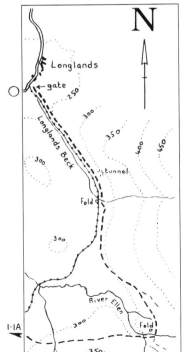

cresting the top of a rise at a little signpost you turn left down the far side of the hedge for a few yards to a stile and gate. Now the path heads diagonally across the field to the bottom of a wood and a little bridge over a stream.

The next field contains a large square earthwork which was once thought to be a Roman camp. It may be the garth of an early medieval settlement, but is more likely only twelfth century, for in those times it was fashionable to own a moated farmstead as an indication of wealth and status.

Beyond the earthwork lies a gated bridge and the hedge is followed to the lane where a stone pillar crowned with a carved head sports a top hat. Overwater Hall, now a hotel, is a cross between an ice-cream parlour and a castle. It was built in 1840 after the original Whitfield House was demolished and has an impressive coat of arms over the porticoed entrance. Turning right along the tarmac track past Pond Cottage, turn right again along the road to the start of the walk.

1.1B

WALK 1.2: SCALES TARN AND BOWSCALE FELL

Tarns:	Scales Tarn
	Bowscale Tarn
Distance:	9 miles
Ascent:	2050ft
Summary:	Easy mountain walking to two corrie tarns and the summit of Bowscale Fell. The featureless fell top is confusing in mist.
Starting Point:	(GR 363305) Mungrisdale, ample parking by the roadside.

High on the eastern slopes of Blencathra, under the impressive wall of rock whose crest is Sharp Edge, Scales Tarn has all the presence and atmosphere of the mountain tarns of central Lakeland. Yet these rocks, for all their rugged qualities, are still the same crumbling slates that make up the whole of the Skiddaw Range, harder perhaps than the rest, but ancient sediments laid down on the sea bed over 500 million years ago. These are the oldest rocks in the Lake District.

Long before the dinosaurs appeared, the slates that make up these crags were transformed. Raised and folded under incredible force by the intrusion of a huge mass of granite forced up from within the earth, the slate was altered by the great heat of the molten lava, driving off the water contained within the crystals and hardening the rock. And it is because of this increased hardness that the crags appear, for as the glaciers smoothed the surrounding mountains into their uniform rounded shapes, the harder rocks resisted until they stood out as cliffs.

While the fells Back o'Skiddaw were once heather covered grouse moors, these eastern tops, which have been sheep walks for centuries, are more often grassy slopes. The hardened slate appears again in Bannerdale Crags, but no tarn lies at the foot of these cliffs and it is not until the edge of Bowscale Fell, above the valley of the infant River Caldew, that the other impressive tarn appears. Like Scales Tarn the cliffs are called Tarn Crags, but facing north these waters shun the sunlight even more. Wordsworth incorporated into a poem the legendary pair of immortal fish that lived in the tarn, and looking down on its dark surface one can imagine how William Hutchinson in the 1770s believed the locals who said that often at mid-day they saw the stars reflected. But the conditions required are seldom found, for "In order to discover that phenomenon, the firmament must be perfectly clear, the air stable, and the water unagitated".

It had been a good walk, but as the afternoon drew on, the clouds lowered onto the fells and the first drops of rain began to fall. The view closed in and soon it was pouring with rain. Slowly we came down the fellside

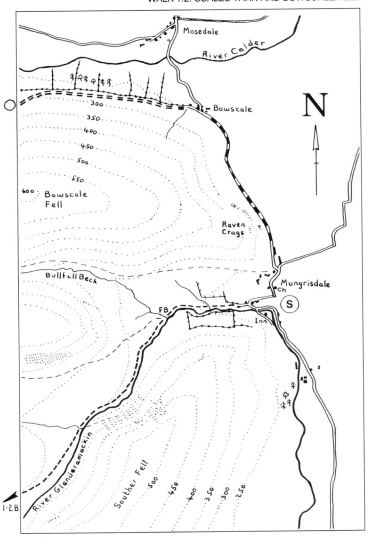

Mosedale

River Calder

Bowscale

350
400
450
500
550
600

Bowscale
Fell

Raven
Crags

Bullfell Beck

Mungrisdale
Ch

S

FB

Inn

River Glenderamackin

Souther Fell

500 450 400 350 300 250

1·2 B

N

1.2A

Atkinson Pike

towards the River Caldew and Mosedale. Below us were the night-black waters of Bowscale Tarn, but of the stars there was not a sign.

ROUTE DESCRIPTION

Glenderamackin River

From the centre of Mungrisdale, which is named after St Kentigern, the eighth-century bishop of Glasgow also somewhat confusingly known as St Mungo, a public footpath sets off past the telephone box. It is a rough track leading up into the hills, but after crossing Bullfell Beck you leave the main path to continue beside the River Glenderamackin. Passing beneath the arc of Bannerdale Crags, which is divided in two by a long central spur, the old mine road climbs on by the diminishing river, and to the left rise the steep slopes of Souther Fell.

Souther Fell is famed for its phantom army, for on Midsummer Eve in 1735 the servant of William Lancaster saw soldiers marching along the crest. Exactly two years later, to the day, William Lancaster himself and all his family saw the army and then in 1745 the troops, this time accompanied by coaches, were seen by some 26 people. Yet although Souther Fell was searched for tracks, no sign of their passing could be found, and the apparition has never been seen again.

Scales Tarn (*The tarn by the hut*)
As the path swings round below White Horse Bent the river must be crossed at the footbridge, then slanting back, a higher path is joined on the far side of the Glenderamackin valley. This path now contours along the hillside and ahead, rising to the point of Atkinson Pike, is Sharp Edge, the most challenging way to Blencathra's summit.

Scales Tarn is an out and back, but reaching Brunt Knott a clear path climbs steeply beside Scales Beck to the tarn. It is a delightful spot, the black water ringed by steep rocks, and high above the tiny figures of walkers are silhouetted against the sky on Sharp Edge. This tarn vies with Bowscale Tarn as the inspiration for the "sable tarn" in Sir Walter Scott's poem *The Bridal of Triermain* where the sun never shines, and at noon its surface reflects the stars.

Bowscale Fell (*The bow-shaped mountain by the hut*)
Retrace your steps to where the path crosses Scales Beck, and make your way left across a steep, black, shaley slope to rejoin the valley path. The white streaks to be found in the rocks are graptolites, fossils of some of the oldest creatures on earth, and on the far side of the river is Saddleback Old Mine, which was worked for lead in the mid-nineteenth century.

In half a mile the head of the valley and the river's source is reached where you turn right to climb, just east of north, on a faint path heading straight for the little bump on the skyline, the summit of Bowscale Fell. The narrow uncairned path makes a beeline for the top over the rather boggy featureless moor, while glancing back to the right the escarpment of Bannerdale Crags is well seen. The highest point of Bowscale Fell (2303ft) is marked by a horseshoe-shaped wind shelter, but though the cairn just a few paces beyond is a little lower, it gives better views. To the north-west, burnt strips alternating with purple heather on the slopes of Knott show it is still being managed as a grouse moor.

Bowscale Tarn
From the summit the path continues north-east, then in a couple of hundred yards a small cairn to the left marks the descent. A grassy rib leads easily down northwards and Bowscale Tarn, the home of Wordsworth's two immortal fish, soon comes into view beneath Tarn Crags. Ahead, down in the valley, is the Carrock Mine, the only wolfram mine in Cumbria. The workings

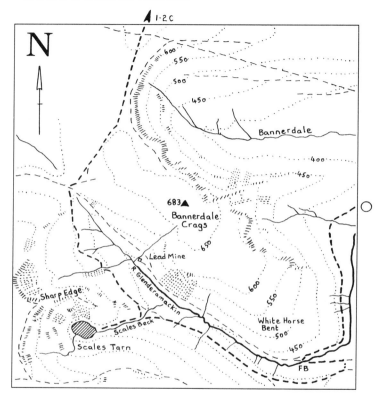

1.2B

have now been tidied up but the mine was in operation from 1854, mainly in times of war, until it finally closed in 1981.

Though a zigzag path short-cuts steeply down a grassy rake straight to the foot of the tarn, it is easier to continue down the gentle hillslope. Resisting the temptation to turn off too soon, continue till you are below the crags and then follow one of the sheep trods that contour round the hill to the tarn. Trapped in a mountain corrie by Ice Age debris, this is the bleak tarn of which Bishop Nicholson wrote in 1703 "So cold y nothing lives in it. Fish have been put in: But they presently dy".

Mungrisdale Cottage

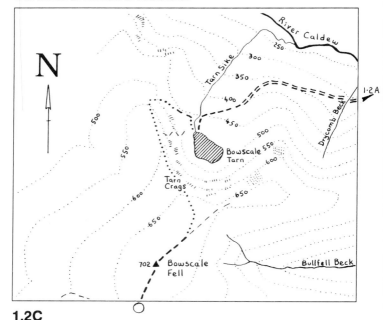

1.2C

Mungrisdale (*The valley of the pigs by St Mungo's church*)
Following the outflow of Tarn Sike, a wide path materialises and this leads
gently downhill towards the River Caldew. On the other side of the river lies
the long grey shape of Carrock Fell, which was climbed by Charles Dickens
in the company of Wilkie Collins. It was a miserable day and Dickens wrote
that from the summit they got "a magnificent view of - Nothing!"

The track follows the intake wall out to the road where you turn right
under the slopes of Bowscale Fell back to Mungrisdale. This attractive little
village has a small church, dating from 1756, with an unusual three-decker
pulpit, but perhaps the inn, named after a water-mill which stopped working
early in the nineteenth century, may be even more welcome.

WALK 1.3: TEWET TARN AND HIGH RIGG

Tarns:	Tewet Tarn
	High Rigg Tarn
	Snipeshow Tarn
Distance:	7 miles
Ascent:	1250ft
Summary:	A walk from Castlerigg Stone Circle over one of Lakeland's attractive lower fells.
Starting Point:	(GR 292238) 1 mile east of Keswick by Castlerigg Stone Circle. Roadside parking.

To the tarn hunter High Rigg is a tease. Sometimes the fell is all come-hither, with sparkling little pools enticing with coquettish glances, on the next occasion it is in a bad mood, with downcast eyes, sulking looks and not a gleam of water to be seen. In a wet year, with up to a dozen pools, there is plenty on High Rigg to occupy an afternoon, but a single visit is misleading and in many a summer only patches of dried mud mock the hopeful suitor. Yet on the southern extremity of the ridge, tucked away behind a rocky knoll, is an attractive and dependable tarn where bog asphodel is a splash of bright gold among the rushes and burr reeds that fringe the water.

There is no dispute, though, about Snipeshow Tarn. How could there be? For after all it has a name. But set a little aloof from the Naddle valley and

Castlerigg Stone Circle

the ever busy A591 it is an inconstant creature. We climbed the fellside through deep heather and bracken, past the little crags and down to the hollow where Snipeshow Tarn lay. But it had gone. Of the pool, deep enough for a swim on our previous visit, there was not a sign. Only a few whitened stones, some dried mud, and the boulder, against which we had seen wavelets splash, told the tale of what had been.

But wet or dry, Tewet Tarn is always there. The name comes from peewit, the birds whose black and white plumage and tumbling flight as they wheel and call above their nests is a delight of spring on the moor, while mirrored in its waters is Blencathra.

Between Tewet Tarn and High Rigg is the church of St John's in the Vale and the grave of John Richardson, the dialect poet. Born in 1817 he became a mason like his father and built the parsonage, the school and also rebuilt the church, doing much of the work himself. Schooled by Edward Wilson the curate, he received a good enough education to become the schoolmaster in 1858 and his poem *Its nobbut me* is still remembered with affection.

Dialect poetry is perhaps a minority interest these days, and St John's in the Vale, the name of the valley as well as the church, is better known for the Castle Rock of Triermain. It is certainly well known by rock climbers for the cliff, which is not just vertical but actually overhangs throughout its entire height, has some very high standard climbs. Yet the fame, and even the name of the rock, was established by Sir Walter Scott in 1805 with his epic poem *The Bridal of Triermain* which tells how the knight, Sir Roland, storms the enchanted castle in his quest for the daughter of King Arthur and the Fairy Queen.

> *Paled in by many a lofty hill,*
> *The narrow dale lay smooth and still,*
> *And, down its verdant bosom led,*
> *A winding brooklet found its bed.*
> *But, midmost of the vale, a mound*
> *Arose with airy turrets crown'd,*
> *Buttress, and rampire's circling bound,*
> *And mighty keep and tower;*

The castle is, alas, fictional, but there is nothing unreal about Castlerigg Stone Circle. Southey, who became Poet Laureate in 1813, was rather dismissive of Castlerigg, "The circle is of the rudest kind, consisting of single stones, unhewn, and chosen without any regard to shape or magnitude", but the 38 stones which make a circle 100ft in diameter, and ten more forming a rectangle on the east side, are an impressive sight. It was late in the afternoon as we came back across the fields, the reddening sun cast long shadows across the fell, and the ancient stones standing as black silhouettes under the gaze of Blencathra had all the magic and mystery of an enchanted age.

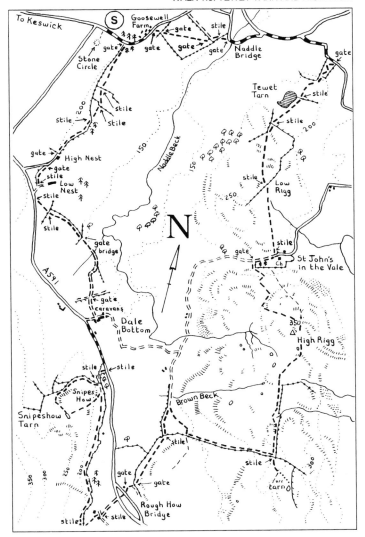

1.3

ROUTE DESCRIPTION

Tewet Tarn (*Peewit Tarn*)

The lane, once the main road to Penrith and improved by the great Mr McAdam in 1824, leads past the field containing Castlerigg Stone Circle and down to Goosewell Farm. Opposite the farm a footpath goes straight across the fields and the road is joined again at Naddle Bridge, the bridge of the wedge-shaped valley. Then with the view to the left dominated by the great buttresses of Blencathra, the road leads uphill. Turn right at the next two junctions, and after about half a mile of tarmac, the highest point is reached where a public footpath leads off to the right.

Climbing steadily the grassy path winds up the hillside through a gateway, past a little quarry, then Tewet Tarn comes into view. A step stile crosses the wall to the left of the tarn which, when it is calm and serene, mirrors the slopes of Blencathra, though on all our visits half a gale has been blowing. The tarn is about 5ft deep and as well as containing native small perch, has been stocked with rainbow and brown trout for the local fishermen.

High Rigg (*High ridge*)

Crossing a wooden stile the path traverses the grassy felltop of Low Rigg to another stile over the stone wall, then descends to the little church of St John's in the Vale which is almost hidden in the trees. Inside is a display about John Richardson, the dialect poet and most famous son of the parish, who also built many of the nineteenth-century houses in Keswick.

The lane, once an important road from Matterdale to the Naddle valley, leads past the old school which is now incorporated into the Carlisle Diocesan Youth Centre, then after a small plantation you turn left up the fellside. The climb is short but steep, zigzagging up the grassy slope, and soon the highest point appears ahead. High Rigg is not much over a thousand feet, but there is an extensive view. To the north Tewet Tarn can be seen on its grassy shelf, and above it are the high Northern Fells with the steep gullies of Blencathra, Lonscale Fell and the mighty Skiddaw, while eastward lies Bram Crag and the lower slopes of the Helvellyn Range.

High Rigg Tarn

Most of the tarns on High Rigg are small seasonal pools which soon dry up and only one is a permanent stretch of water. Retrace your steps down the summit knoll and then head southwards along the ridge high above St John's in the Vale, where in the distance you can see the "airy turrets" of Castle Rock. Reaching the wall corner follow the wall along, skirting a boggy area, to a ladder stile. The next section is an out and back. Continue at first in the same direction, then as Raven Crag appears dramatically ahead, and the path sets off downhill, climb leftwards, round behind the rocky knoll to reach the little tarn which lies beside the fence. Fringed with spike-rush and bogbean, there are patches of bog asphodel, and in July its tiny island was one golden mass of lesser spearwort.

Snipeshow Tarn (*Snipes hill tarn*)
Returning to the ladder stile a narrow path, somewhat overgrown with bracken, follows the wall down. Near the bottom of the fell the path bends away from the wall to join the valley track where you go left along the bridleway to Rough How Bridge and across a narrow strip of field to the main road. Crossing the busy A591 take the track, a public footpath, towards Shoulthwaite Farm, and at the bend go over the stile. "Thwaite" shows the Norse origins of the place, and this was the clearing with the mill-wheel.

At the top of the field is a ladder stile, and turning right the path now follows the far side of the wall to pass above Brackenrigg. Snipeshow Tarn hides rather shyly on the fellside and is best found by turning off just before the field gate, where a faint path doubles back beneath Snipes How to climb to the tiny tarn cupped in a hollow. To the north Skiddaw is framed in the V-shape above the outflow, and while on our visit we were disappointed to find the tarn completely dry, on another occasion there was frog-spawn in the outflow and the large rock was an unreachable island.

Castlerigg (*Castle ridge*)
From the north end of the tarn a little path leads round the far side of Snipes How to meet a wall and this is followed down to rejoin the main path. Going through a field gate and beside the wood, the main road is reached. There is now an unavoidable quarter mile of road walking to Dale Bottom, but fortunately there is a grassy verge.

Turning into the farm entrance go left through the caravan park and keep straight on across the fields. Beyond the bridge the track becomes a path and this continues up the side of the field and out to the main road by the entrance to Low Nest Farm.

A few yards along the farm track, and after the cattle-grid, the footpath goes over a stile to follow the edge of the field and then joins a track to the whitewashed buildings of High Nest. Passing the house the route continues through the meadows over a series of ladder stiles to emerge on the lane beside the Stone Circle. Described by Keats as a "dismal cirque of Druid Stone upon a forlorn moor", it was purchased in 1913 by Canon Rawnsley for the National Trust.

WALK 1.4: CARLSIDE TARN

Tarn:	Carlside Tarn
Distance:	6 miles
Ascent:	2400ft
	(Visiting Skiddaw summit adds on 1 ½ miles and 650ft of ascent)
Summary:	A steep ascent followed by a superb ridge walk, with a return by St Bega's church.
Starting Point:	(GR 236281) Dodd Wood car park, 3 miles north of Keswick on the A591. Cafe, toilets.

In Skiddaw Slate country, tarns are pretty rare things, so even after the 2000ft climb that is required to reach it, one must not complain that Carlside Tarn is not much to look at. Little more than a large puddle in the hollow between the grassy dome of Carl Side and the bare grey stony southern slopes of Skiddaw, it is only a few inches deep. But whatever Carlside Tarn lacks in appearance, there is more than recompense in its surroundings, for the ridge of Ullock Pike and Longside Edge is one of the most delightful walks in the Northern Fells, and if extended to take in the summit of Skiddaw itself, then this is a far finer way to Lakeland's elder statesman of a mountain than the usual trudge up the wide track from Latrigg.

"Excuse me" said the man, "but what mountain is this?" In the low cloud and steady drizzle stood someone who had clearly taken the wrong turn in Keswick. Dressed in a lounge suit and shiny Oxford shoes, he was descending the steep scree slope from the summit of Skiddaw to Carl Side. It is more usual to find incongruous attire on the other side of the mountain, where beachwear, sandals and flip-flops are as often encountered as boots. But "Skiddaw's lofty height", which Wordsworth saw as a boy from Cockermouth, with its massive dominant shape rising above the busy Keswick streets, has long drawn people to the top.

The first written account comes in 1684 with the ascent by Bishop Nicholson, and the names of many famous people are linked with the mountain. William Wilberforce, the anti-slavery campaigner, made an ascent in 1779, Charles and Mary Lamb in 1802, while Coleridge had the surprise of meeting an admirer of his on the top. John Keats and Charles Brown, on their walking tour in 1818, believing in early starts set off at 4am, but none of these equalled the festivities held to celebrate Nelson's victory at Waterloo.

Keswick was determined to do things in style, and on the evening of 21st August 1815 the summit of Skiddaw saw a large crowd assembled there including Wordsworth, draped in a borrowed red cloak, his wife Mary, their 12-year old son John, and Robert Southey. As a great fire of tar barrels

Skiddaw from Ashness Bridge, Borrowdale

roared up into the sky they ate roast beef and plum puddings, consumed a huge bowl of punch and then, after singing the National Anthem and drinking toasts punctuated by volleys of shots from a cannon, proceeded to roll flaming balls of tow and turpentine down the mountain. According to Southey "The effect was grand beyond imagination".

It was Wordsworth who caused the festivities to become even more riotous. The "water-drinking bard", whose strict abstinence once led Sir Walter Scott to creep out of the window at Dove Cottage to visit the pub, tripped over the kettle and with nothing to dilute it, the rum punch was consumed neat by the party. Everyone got very joyful, and at the end of the evening one of the guests had to be carried down slung over the back of a horse.

Ours was a more sober descent, and as we reached the valley the sun came out. Hats, gloves and waterproofs, which had kept out the bitter wind of the mountain summit, were soon discarded and we strolled across the fields to St Bega's church, enclosed within its circular stone wall. Just beyond is the shore of Bassenthwaite Lake and we remembered Alfred Lord Tennyson's words from *Morte D'Arthur*, written on this shore in 1836 when staying at nearby Mirehouse: "I heard the water lapping on the crag and the long ripple washing in the reeds". The wind sighed in the trees and on the lake little waves chased each other across the water, but inside the church all was quiet and still.

ROUTE DESCRIPTION

Dodd Wood (*Wood on the bare, round hill*)

From the Old Saw Mill, which was built around 1880 and is now a cafe, a bridge leads over Skill Beck and a footpath zigzags up to join the forest road. It is then a steady climb through the trees until the col is gained between Dodd and Carl Side. The Forestry Commission started work here in the 1920s, but this part of the wood was first planted with conifers in 1790 by Thomas Story of Mirehouse.

Carl Side (*Karl's hill slope*)

At the col a step stile on the left leads to a steep, narrow fell path through bracken, heather and some of the finest and biggest bilberries in the Lakes. These must have been appreciated by the Skiddaw Hermit who lived on Dodd in the 1800s and earned his living by painting portraits.

Soon Derwent Water comes into view, and the ridge path from Millbeck is joined at the outcrop of White Stones. The path continues steeply uphill and to the right is the large grey mass of Skiddaw Little Man, looking much more impressive than Skiddaw itself. It's a head down plod, until as the 600m contour is passed the angle begins to ease and the path leads straight to the rather insignificant cairn on the summit of Carl Side (2447ft). Skiddaw now

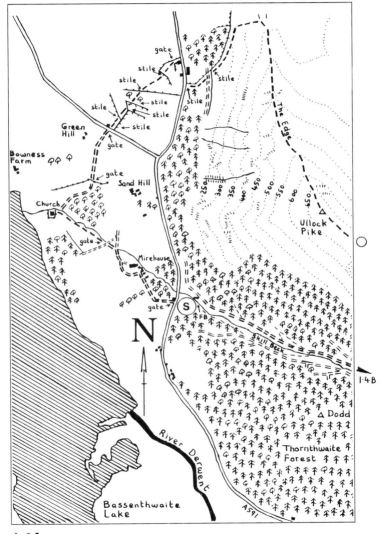

1.4A

assumes its true proportions and the best views are southwards towards Borrowdale and the central Lakeland fells.

Carlside Tarn

The path, surprisingly indistinct, continues north-eastwards to the grassy col where Carlside Tarn is to be found. Hardly deserving of so grand a name, this very shallow, lozenge-shaped pool beneath the grey inhospitable screes of Skiddaw, disappears in dry weather. If it is a good day you may be tempted by the steep path which climbs north-eastwards to the 3000ft summit of Skiddaw, but then return by the same route to continue over Long Side.

Long Side (*Long hill slope*)

From Carlside Tarn a good path heads westward high above the green and empty expanse of Southerndale, and it is only a short climb to the top of Long Side (2408ft) where you look down on Dodd and across the valley of the Derwent to the North Western Fells. To the north-east the summit cairn of Skiddaw is silhouetted against the sky.

Ullock Pike (*The peak by where the wolves play*)

It is a lovely promenade along the airy ridge ("it's a pity it isn't much longer" said Wainwright) and with only the briefest of climbs, the summit of Ullock Pike (2264ft) is reached. Far below is Bassenthwaite Lake, strictly the only 'lake' in the Lake District for all the others are 'waters' or 'meres', and since 1979 it has been owned by the Lake District Special Planning Board. In the patchwork of green fields beside the lake you can just pick out St Bega's church. Though much of the building is Victorian restoration, the site is very old and the first worshippers would have arrived by boat.

It is now a delightfully easy stroll down The Edge until drawing level with the end of the forest you leave the ridge and descend to join the path beside the trees. This leads down to a little gate into the wood where you cross a forest track and descend very steeply to the busy main road beside the grounds of the Ravenstone Hotel.

St Bega's Church

Turn right along the road as far as the hotel entrance and take the footpath to the left over the fields and through a little wood, then crossing the tarmac lane follow the track which skirts round Highfield Wood to St Bega's church.

St Bega was the daughter of an Irish chieftain in the seventh century who vowed to remain celibate and dedicate her life to God. Her father, however, arranged for her to marry the son of the King of Norway so she fled to Cumberland to St Bees Head, where she founded a nunnery to care for the sick and the poor. Although the church which dates back to the tenth century was restored in 1874, only four years later a second church was built nearer

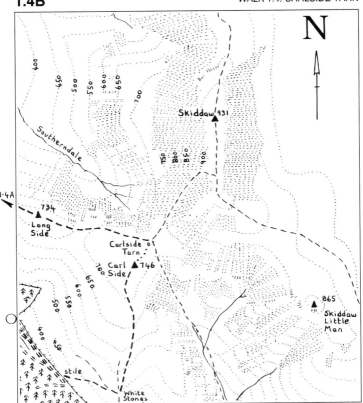

N

to Bassenthwaite village.

There is little sign of the path to Mirehouse, but keeping to the right of Skill Beck a kissing gate leads to a track past the seventeenth-century hall which was built as a hunting lodge by the Earl of Derby. In 1802 the house was left to John Spedding of Armathwaite Hall who was at school in Hawkshead with Wordsworth. The house has further literary connections for John's youngest son James was a close friend of both Tennyson and Thomas Carlyle. The track continues past the kitchen garden and the main road is reached opposite the Old Saw Mill. If you set out early, like Mr John Adams the cartographer who in 1689 recommended an early morning start "to avoid the sun on one's back during the ascent", you should be just in time for tea.

2: Patterdale Tarns

WALK 2.1: RED TARN AND BROWN COVE

Tarns:	Lanty's Tarn
	Red Tarn
	Brown Cove Tarn
Distance:	8 miles
Ascent:	2150ft
Summary:	Easy mountain walking round the lower slopes of Helvellyn.
Starting Point:	(GR 386170) Glenridding village at the southern end of Ullswater. Large car park, toilets.

Ten thousand years ago the ice began to melt. The corrie glaciers that had grown in the eastern recesses of Helvellyn started to shrink, and the ice which had spilled down the valley towards Glenridding at last drew back. It was the end of the Ice Age. Gradually the icy tongues retreated, until at last the piles of debris, rocks and boulders heaped up by the glaciers were exposed, while behind these barriers the ice continued to melt in the hollows that were to become Red Tarn, Brown Cove Tarn, and the tarn of Kepple Cove.

And so the tarns remained through the Stone Age, the Bronze Age and the Iron Age, and through the centuries of recorded history right up to the year 1927.

It was hard work getting up at 4am, and even harder work making the climb to Kepple Cove, but the miner, whose job it was to turn on the water, was used to early starts, late finishes and heavy labour. The Glenridding Mine needed water, and though it was a profitable undertaking, one of the most profitable in the Lake District, power was expensive and a ready supply of water was a major asset for any mine.

Water-wheels had been used for over a century to power pumps, winding machinery and processing engines, and the Glenridding Mine was one of the most advanced in the country. Turbines had been installed to replace the less efficient water-wheels and it was the first metalliferous mine in the country to employ electrical power and run generators that supplied winding gear, compressors and even an underground railway.

All this on water power. But one October night in 1927 came disaster. The miners had improved on nature, piling earth and stones onto the moraine dam until it stood some 30ft above its original height, while a pipe had been drilled under the dam to tap an even lower level. But all night the rain fell and

Winter at Red Tarn, Helvellyn

the water poured into the tarn. At one o'clock in the morning the dam could hold no longer.

Asleep in Glenridding, no-one knew until the tidal wave hit them. A wall of water roared down Glenridding Beck, and a mass of 25,000 tons of rock and a quarter of a million gallons of water travelling at the speed of an express train hurtled into the village. Families found themselves afloat in their beds, doors were broken open just in time to save the occupants and the debris spilled out into the lake forming a new headland. Miraculously no-one was killed, and in half an hour it was all over. The devastation was immense and the recompense paid by the owners nearly ruined the mine. But the tarn that for thousands of years had lain under the slopes of Helvellyn was gone. Kepple Cove Tarn was no more.

"I think you're marvellous!" The speaker was a young lady we had just overtaken on the climb from Patterdale to Striding Edge, and as she and her companions turned aside on reaching Hole-in-the-Wall to descend towards Red Tarn, we climbed on, towards the narrow crest that leads to Helvellyn. It was December and while the sun, out of a clear blue sky, warmed the rocks, on the dark, shadowed side of the ridge, ice and hoar frost glistened blue. We were on a backpacking trip. Our rucksacks stuffed with winter sleeping bags, stove, food and mountain tent, with crampons and ice axes strapped securely to the outside, we were planning to camp high on the frozen summit.

"Marvellous!" We felt good. Perhaps our pace increased just a little, the packs felt lighter too. The sun shone and above us Helvellyn beckoned. It was a perfect day. It was then that a nagging suspicion dawned. "Marvellous!" Wasn't that one of those patronising remarks made to the elderly? We looked down, far below the tiny specks of the distant girl and her friends stood beside Red Tarn. But they were going down, we were going up. What did it matter? We felt marvellous anyway.

ROUTE DESCRIPTION

Lanty's Tarn (*Lancelot's Tarn*)

On the far side of Glenridding Beck a private road goes past the shops, and then in 300 yards forks left, signed "Lanty Tarn and Helvellyn". Passing the cottages to go left over a footbridge, the path then climbs through a wood, zigzagging up the hillside to the plantation which almost surrounds Lanty's Tarn.

The tarn, which was named after Lancelot Dobson who lived in the valley below, was enlarged by the Marshall family who rebuilt Patterdale Hall in 1824. When employment was scarce, William Marshall paid local men to make the pony tracks on this hillside and on his estate. Although the view is restricted by the trees, from the dam you can look up the long Grisedale valley, while a short detour to the summit of the little hill of Keldas above the tarn gives a bird's-eye view of Glenridding village and the lake.

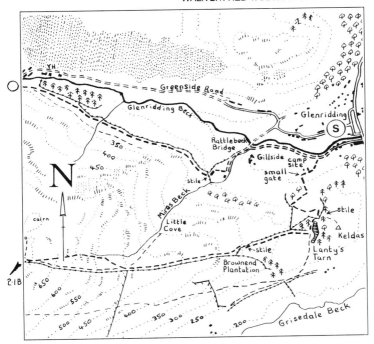

2.1A

Birkhouse Moor (*Birch house moor*)

From the tarn, head uphill across the open ground following the edge of the plantation, and then the wall, to a stone step stile. Continuing on the other side the path climbs steeply beside the wall, and the view gradually expands to include the head of Ullswater. After an easy plod up steep grassy slopes, the main route from Little Cove is joined, and the path is diverted away from the wall.

On reaching the ridge, Helvellyn, Striding Edge, and the pointed top of Catstye Cam appear ahead, but though a cairn on the spur which projects northwards looks a tempting top with a fine view of the valley, the true summit of Birkhouse Moor (2356ft) is by the wall.

Red Tarn

It is an easy stroll beside the wall to the ladder stile at Hole-in-the-Wall where the ridge sets off uphill again. Keen walkers who want to climb Helvellyn can add on the classic round of Striding Edge and Swirral Edge, but for the direct route to Red Tarn take the broad path forking off to the right. This descends gently, only to peter out after half a mile in a mound of glacial moraine, a natural dam which until the last moment hides the tarn.

Red Tarn, held in its wild and lonely corrie under the cliffs of Helvellyn, with tumbled bare rocks and boulders scattered upon its shore, appears almost bleak in summer and even the experts list only four plants in its waters, but in winter it is magnificent. And winter can last a long time as Wordsworth's lines record:

> It was a cove, a huge recess,
> That keeps, till June, December's snow;
> A lofty precipice in front,
> A silent tarn below.

High above, tiny figures are silhouetted against the sky on the crests of Striding Edge and Swirral Edge, while on the summit of Helvellyn you can just pick out the trig point.

The tarn, which as well as trout is said to contain the schelly, a rare kind of fresh-water herring, is dammed by glacial moraine which was raised in 1840 to supply water to the mines. But the dam has now been breached and Red Tarn Beck escapes through the gap, leaving the stone-walled culvert completely dry.

Brown Cove Tarn

On the far side of the beck the main path comes down from Swirral Edge, and this is followed down beside a series of pretty cascades. After nearly ³/₄ mile, at about the 530m contour, an artificial watercourse crosses the hillside marked by a line of rushes. This was constructed in 1890 to supply the turbines of the power station in the valley, and provides a convenient route round the lower slopes of Catstye Cam to Brown Cove. The line of the watercourse is generally clear, and though a few rotting timbers are all that remain of an aqueduct round a rocky knoll, further on the wooden launder is well preserved.

After about a mile the leat joins Glenridding Beck by the stone slipway of an ugly concrete dam, which is rent by a huge gash from top to bottom. This was High Dam which collapsed in 1931, only four years after the Keppel Cove disaster and again, miraculously, there was no loss of life in the valley below. Follow the slipway up then climb through old mine workings above the dam to join a little trod which rounds the hillside. On the far side of the beck is the breached Kepple Cove Dam.

Brown Cove Tarn, now shrunken to its original size, was extended in 1860 to serve the lead mines and there is an untidy jumble of stones and the remains of a dam at its lower end. Surrounded by the steep slopes of Catstye

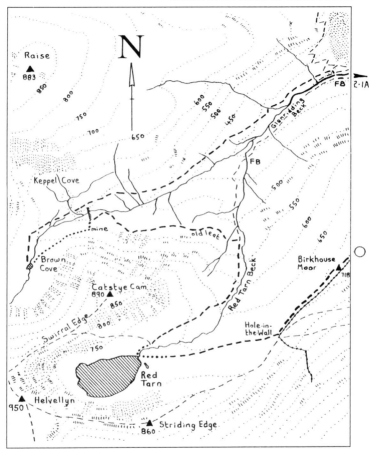

2.1B

Cam, Helvellyn Lower Man and White Side, the setting is dramatic, but the tarn is little visited, a remote spot well off the beaten track. In contrast to the surroundings of Red Tarn, there is an oasis of fertile ground between the becks where the bowling green turf is sprinkled with purple thyme.

Greenside Mine (*Green hillslope mine*)

Crossing over the ruined dam, the path is joined on the other side of the stream where stone channels diverted water into Keppel Cove. Beyond the huge 100ft-wide gash in the peat and stone dam, a track starts by the sheepfolds and keeping high above the stream, descends to Greenside Mine. As the path draws near to the lead mines there is a well preserved system of old leats, then just before the buildings you cross the metal footbridge.

In 1868 the mines were regarded by guidebook writers as an added attraction on the climb to Helvellyn, which enhanced the tourist's enjoyment. "The whole of the ore-crushing, washing and smelting processes can be inspected. The mines....command a fine view of Patterdale." But only 23 years later Baddeley wrote of "the one blot on Patterdale's otherwise perfect loveliness" and Ruskin and Canon Rawnsley took up the cause to prevent further despoilation of the Lakes.

Glenridding (*Valley in the bracken*)

Taking the lower path, follow the wall beside the wood. Across the valley are the old mine buildings which have been converted to a youth hostel and an outdoor activities centre. After the mine closed in 1962 the spoil heaps were covered with sludge from a sewage farm at Penrith to help plants gain a hold, but recovery of the landscape is a slow process.

After a mile the track is joined at a ladder stile and followed downhill. Turn right just before Rattlebeck Bridge, once the site of the power station, and follow the path beside the river through the campsite and back to Glenridding. There are plans to generate hydro-electric power from the Greenside site again to supply electricity to the village, and soon the old power house will be in use once more.

WALK 2.2: HARD TARN AND NETHERMOST PIKE

Tarns:	Hard Tarn
	Grisedale Tarn
Distance:	9$\frac{1}{2}$ miles
Ascent:	2850ft
	(Visiting the summit of Helvellyn adds on 1$\frac{1}{2}$ miles and 350ft)
Summary:	A secret tarn in a pathless, hidden valley, then a steep scramble up Nethermost Pike to join the tourist trail down to Grisedale Tarn.

Hard Tarn

Starting Point: (GR 390161) Patterdale at the southern end of Ullswater.
                     Parking for a few cars at the beginning of the lane to
                     Grisedale. Car park and toilets ½ mile down the road in
                     Patterdale village.

One of the most elusive of all mountain tarns, and reached only after a steep
climb to an isolated combe, Hard Tarn clings to a narrow shelf high on the
eastern slopes of Nethermost Pike. Held by a natural dam of naked rock, with
above it rough scree and rock buttresses presenting an unscaleable wall, no
paths converge upon it, and the tarn sees few visitors, but the setting is
magnificent, a lone and secret place facing the rising sun.

These fells with an unrestricted eastwards view are a favourite for
watchers of the dawn, and every summer the summit of Helvellyn is a place
of pilgrimage for many who spend the night huddled uncomfortably in bivvy
bags around the cairn waiting for the first gleam of day, but even finer is the
sunrise in winter.

It was late and hoar frost sparkled among the shadows as we approached
the summit of Dollywaggon Pike, and though, in the still air, the evening felt
warm as we pitched our little tent beside the cairn, the ground was solid ice.
Gradually the sun sank towards the Scafells and the western hills became
black silhouettes against a fiery sky streaked with orange and red, while
below us the mist flowed in, filling the valleys with a thick white vapour. The
call of a raven echoed back from the rocks as it glided in to settle on the cliffs,
and as a gentle breeze stirred the tent we retired into our warm down sleeping
bags. Soon the stars began to appear and as the sky slowly darkened into
night we looked up at Orion, the Plough, and the faint misty gleam of the Milky
Way.

The advantage of watching the dawn in winter is that the sun rises at a
very civilised hour, and it was well past eight o'clock when we emerged from
our tent. Around us was a white sea and rising like islands were Bow Fell,
Gable and the Scafells, just black shapes against the gradually paling night.
Not a whisper of a breeze stirred. In the west a few stars still shone, but
beyond High Street a thin line of light brushed the hills. Slowly, very slowly,
the light became brighter, the hills turned from black to grey, and above us
a thin high streak of cloud glowed orange against the dark sky.

Suddenly there it was, a brilliant speck on the horizon, which as we
watched gradually grew, like a fire, setting the summits alight and scorching
each of the hills with flame. Around us the rocks, the stones, the ice, the
mountains themselves, Nethermost Pike, Helvellyn, the Far Eastern Fells,
all burned in the colours of the dawn, while above the mass of St Sunday
Crag, still wrapped in black shadow, the crest danced with light. With
gathering swiftness the glowing disc grew moment by moment. Soon half of
it was visible, then three-quarters, until at last the sun broke free and rose into
the blinding glare of day.

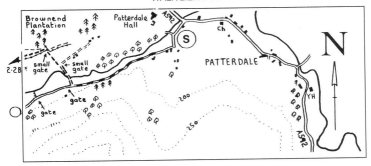

2.2A

ROUTE DESCRIPTION

Ruthwaite Lodge (*Rough clearing lodge*)

A narrow tarmac lane leads uphill beside Grisedale Beck, and to the right among the trees lies Patterdale Hall, the home of John Mounsey, known as the "King of Patterdale" after he defeated a band of marauding Scots in the seventeenth century. The house was rebuilt in 1840 by William Marshall who also planted many rare trees in the grounds.

After half a mile a track on the right, signed "Footpath to Helvellyn", leads across Grisedale Beck, then at the bend keep straight on through a kissing gate and up the field to another little gate by Brownend Plantation. The main route slanting up the fellside is heading for Striding Edge, but instead go left on the lower path which follows the wall. Progress is easy along the flanks of Grisedale, through a series of little metal gates and past Braesteads Farm, set amid the green fields of the valley floor. On the far side of the valley are the stony slopes of St Sunday Crag, and ahead looms Dollywaggon Pike but, above the mine spoil heaps, the route to be followed later up the nose of Nethermost Pike looks impossibly steep.

The path continues past Broomhill Plantation and through the rounded grassy hummocks of a glacial moraine, then crossing a bridge over Nethermostcove Beck it begins to climb by the spoil tips of the disused Eagle Crag lead mine. There are six Eagle Crags in the Lake District, named in the days when the Golden Eagle was more frequently seen, but now the only nesting site is by Haweswater.

Crossing another bridge the two valley paths unite and a little higher is Ruthwaite Lodge. The stone hut, which is used by Sheffield Mountaineering Club, was destroyed by fire some years ago, but in 1992 it was restored and the green slates now cover a new metal-ridged roof. Originally built as an office and mine shop, or barracks, for the Ruthwaite Lodge Mine, there was
45

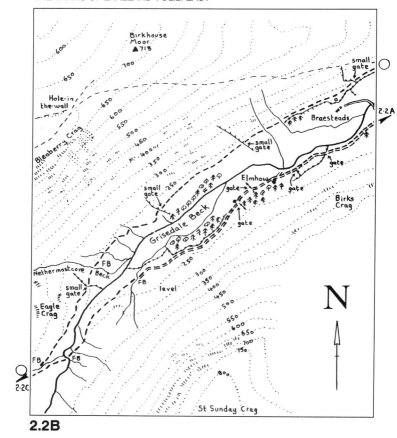

2.2B

also a powder house and a smithy, as well as ore sorting and washing floors. Though some of the mine is very old and dates back to Elizabethan times, it was mainly worked in the nineteenth century and closed about 1877. Down by the stream are the remains of old levels and workings, and at the foot of the waterfall a 150 yard long dark tunnel disappears into the hillside.

Hard Tarn (*Inaccessible tarn*)
From the back of the hut a faint grassy path climbs, twisting between the

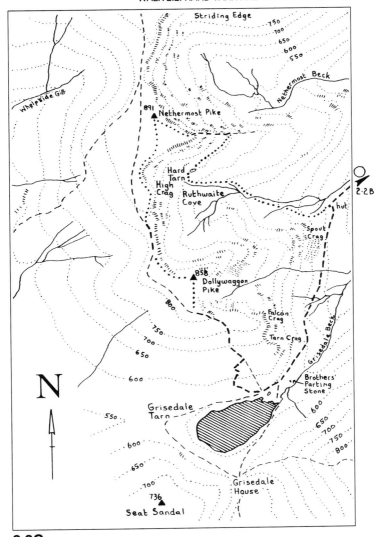

2.2C

rocks, towards Spout Crag before looping back to the stream which is followed up into the hanging valley of Ruthwaite Cove. When the path fades away, cross Ruthwaite Beck and keep to the rightmost tributary up grassy slopes almost into the stony combe ahead. Hard Tarn cannot be seen from below so don't climb too high. It is on the far side of a flat boggy shelf, set on a rock slab under a small cliff, while above steep slopes stretch up to Nethermost Pike. As we sat by the quiet tarn, that feeling of being the only people in the world was shattered by a yellow Mountain Rescue helicopter whirring overhead.

Nethermost Pike (*Lowest peak*)

Having dismissed the thought of a direct ascent of Nethermost Pike, follow the hillside round to a cairn on a large cleft boulder and contour across the rough pathless boulder slope to join the east ridge. Here, surprisingly, there is a path, and the ascent is now straightforward, a steep but easy scramble with the view of Striding Edge expanding to encompass Ullswater and the distant Pennines.

Soon the ridge narrows to a rocky arête, and then climbing the final grassy rib, suddenly the flat mountain top is reached. Feeling perhaps that this is a far finer way to the summit than the boring plod up the tourist path, don't forget to visit the highest point of Nethermost Pike (2923ft). Often ignored by those intent only upon Helvellyn, this is the furthest cairn to the right, beyond the upright stones.

Helvellyn summit is now in view and beyond Striding Edge is the cone of Catstye Cam, while to the west the mountain panorama is magnificent. All the giants of Lakeland are on show, from the Coniston Fells in the south, to the western summits of Bow Fell, Gable and the Scafells, right round to the North Western Fells. It is tempting, when you are so close, to visit the summit of Helvellyn, and the out and back detour along the ridge will add about an extra hour to the walk.

Dollywaggon Pike (*unknown*)

In fine weather the edge of the cliffs can be followed south, with views down into Ruthwaite Cove, but in misty conditions this can be very confusing and it is easier to head west to join the main path. High Crag is deceiving and looks like a separate summit, but the rise beyond, a little way off the path, is the summit of Dollywaggon Pike (2815ft), a narrow grassy promontory marked by a small cairn. Here, after a camp on the summit we once saw that rare mountain vision, a glory, a rainbow of light encircling our shadows on the cloud.

Grisedale Tarn (*The tarn of the pig's valley*)

Following the edge round to join the main path, Grisedale Tarn comes into view in its grassy bowl below. By staying on the old packhorse route which zigzags down the slope, the steep eroded short-cuts are avoided, and soon the shore is reached. The tarn, which is just over 100ft deep, is a popular campsite, with usually one or two tents pitched by the water's edge. Keep a lookout for treasure, as King Dunmail threw the Crown Jewels into Grisedale Tarn when he fled from a battle with the Scots.

The Brothers' Parting Stone

The old packhorse road to Patterdale sets off downhill beside Grisedale Beck, and just below and to the right of the path a rusty notice marks the Brothers' Parting Stone. Here Wordsworth said goodbye to his brother John, captain of the Abergavenny, who was drowned at sea. Eighty years later Canon Rawnsley, the founder of the National Trust, arranged for William's memorial poem to be inscribed on the rock, but the words are now very hard to read and we spent a long time deciphering the verse, which will soon have faded into obscurity.

Patterdale daffodils

> Here did we stop and here looked round,
> While each unto himself descends,
> To that last thought of parting friends,
> That is not to be found.
> Brother and friend, if verse of mine
> Have power to make thy virtues known,
> Here let a monumental stone
> Stand sacred as a shrine.

Grisedale (*Pig's valley*)

Gradually the path descends into the long Grisedale valley and after nearly a mile, once again Ruthwaite Lodge is reached. Continue down past the hut, but don't retrace the outward route, instead take the footbridge and cross Grisedale Beck to follow the main path down on the far side of the valley. On the hillside above is the spoil from a stone-arched trial level, now collapsed, which was part of the Eagle Crag Mine.

After Crossing Plantation the gated track goes by Elmhow Plantation to Elmhow Farm and then, becoming a tarmac lane, it is an easy walk all the way back to Patterdale. If there is time St Patrick's church is worth a visit, with a communion plate and a chalice made out of Helvellyn silver, and in springtime a churchyard full of daffodils.

WALK 2.3: PLACE FELL

Tarns:	Place Fell Tarn
Distance:	7 miles
Ascent:	2000ft
Summary:	An easy fell walk with a return along the most beautiful lakeside path in the Lake District.
Starting Point:	(GR 397158) Patterdale village. Car park, toilets.

"A general discharge of the guns roused us to new astonishment" wrote William Hutchinson in 1772, as the Duke of Portland's boat fired six cannon in quick succession across Ullswater. Echoes were very popular with the tourists, and many eighteenth-century visitors thought the Lake District needed livening up a bit, a view which alas is still widely held and being valiantly resisted by the Planning Board.

Things had quietened down a bit by Victorian times, and in 1957 Wainwright was inspired to write of the lakeside path "the most beautiful and rewarding walk in Lakeland". With such superlatives who could resist? So

The head of Ullswater from Place Fell

despite a discouraging forecast we arrived one July morning in Patterdale, and with large white cumulus clouds towering above the mountains, set off in bright sunshine across the river and beneath the slopes of Place Fell with our baby son sitting happily in his papoose carrier.

As we walked along the lake shore the day grew darker, while over Helvellyn clouds piled upon each other until the sky looked little different from approaching night. The storm was expected, but the first flash of lightning was followed so closely by the thunder that it came as a shock. There had been no rain, but now great heavy drops fell, each one somehow larger and more wetting than ordinary rain. Another flash was followed by an even closer explosion of sound. Perhaps we should wait for it to pass over, and though wanting to run, to get away, we sat down and watched. Curtains of rain swept across the lake, while black clouds boiled overhead. Thor seemed to be getting our range, for the next few minutes were as close to coming under enemy gunfire as we ever want to be. The flash was simultaneous with the deafening bang as we saw lightning hit the ground about 50 yards away. The next was to one side, and then the other. We could no longer sit still. Running away was better. So picking up the baby, who was quite unconcerned by the firework display, we fled. The path round Place Fell has seldom been covered more quickly by a family party.

Sandwick was a haven. In the shelter of a barn we felt comforted, and the closeness of something man-made which must have survived previous storms was reassuring. Gradually the sounds of thunder became more distant and further apart, then venturing again into the open we strode purposefully round Hallin Fell. We arrived panting and breathless at Howtown. On the jetty a handful of people huddled together, while on the lake a group of canoeists paddled happily about. Slowly the steamer edged into the bay. It had been a long walk.

Queen Victoria Jubilee Plate

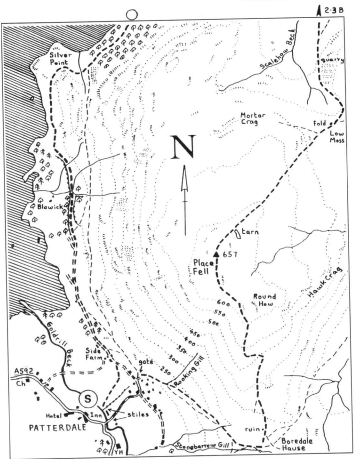

2.3A

ROUTE DESCRIPTION

Boredale Hause (*The pass of the valley with a barn*)

At the south end of Patterdale village, just beyond the White Lion, a narrow tarmac lane leads over Goldrill Bridge to a cluster of houses and Wordsworth Cottage. Though the poet never lived here, he intended to build a house where Broad How now stands and was negotiating to buy the land when Lord Lowther stepped in and bought it for him, but William was embarrassed by his patron's generosity as he thought too high a price had been paid.

Following the road round to the left, turn right through the gate onto the open fellside. The path climbs steeply at first, and then at an easier angle. Keeping to the higher option which passes an old iron seat commemorating Queen Victoria's diamond jubilee, the ascent continues purposefully to Boredale Hause. A multiplicity of paths heads off in all directions, but the leftmost one leads past a rectangular ruin which is all that remains of the Chapel in the Hause. Though now indistinguishable from a sheepfold, these are the ruins of a medieval church, built on the col to serve both Martindale and Patterdale.

Place Fell (*Swampy Mountain*)

Heading north the grassy path climbs steadily, becoming steeper as it rounds a sharp bend. Soon the head of Ullswater and the village of Glenridding come into view, then making a final effort the rocky knoll of Round How with its small cairn is reached. It is now an easy stroll for a further 200 yards over pink stained rocks, and past a substantial wind shelter, to the top.

Place Fell (2155ft), being set apart from other hills, is a fine vantage point and from the stone OS trig point the Helvellyn Range fills the western view, eastwards the skyline is of High Street, and to the south-east lies Wainwright's forbidden summit. Though the Nab is within the Matterdale Deer Sanctuary, there can be few peak-baggers who haven't visited it just once. In winter months Red deer migrate to the slopes of Place Fell, and in very severe weather they even venture into the gardens of Patterdale to find food.

Place Fell Tarn

There are several small pools on the flat fell top, but the only one worth calling a tarn is to the north-east and close by the path. Even this may prove a disappointment, as the large shallow tarn has a tendency to dry up in summer.

The path descends gently north-east, and down past a useful spring to the sheepfold on Low Moss. Then swinging left, you head more steeply down into the valley of Scalehow Beck and past a ruined quarry hut. Keeping to the left fork, where on the boggy slopes the beautiful white petalled grass of Parnassus can be found, the path descends gently to the stream before veering away to join the valley path by a barn.

Ullswater (*Ulf's lake*)

Skirting the fell the path crosses the beck below Scalehow Force then, climbing briefly, continues round the fellside through bracken and tumbled rocks to become a delightful airy route above the lake. On the far side of

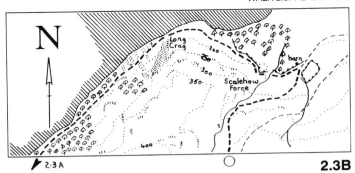

Ullswater, Gowbarrow Fell rises majestically straight from the water's edge, and above the boathouse is the castellated Lyulph's Tower, which Wordsworth tells us was "a pleasure-house built by the late Duke of Norfolk".

As the rocky point of Long Crag is reached the high Eastern Fells come into view above the bend in the lake, and though the summit of Helvellyn is hidden from sight, the pointed top of Catstye Cam is the marker from which all else is identified. Tall juniper bushes and silver birch enclose the path as it contours along the fellside towards the curve of Silver Bay, with its little beach. Then passing Silver Point, Glenridding village appears and the small rocky island of Lingy Holm, which on hot days has tempted us into the lake for a swim.

Climbing a little for the last time the path distances itself from Ullswater and becomes a track. Below is Blowick House, the home of the nineteenth-century painter John Glover, who on emigrating to Tasmania found the inspiration that established him as the first great Australasian artist. At one time, Wordsworth said, wild goats were found here, but a footnote in the 1805 edition of his guide adds that by then they had all disappeared.

After Side Farm, where the Wordsworths often stayed with their friends Captain and Mrs Luff, the lane is unfenced, then a footpath short-cuts across the field to a kissing gate by Goldrill Beck and the bridge back into Patterdale village.

WALK 2.4: CAUDALE MOOR AND BROTHERS WATER

Tarns:	Caudale Moor Tarn
	Brothers Water
Distance:	5¹/₂ miles
Ascent:	2000ft
Summary:	A steep ascent to Hartsop Dodd, then easy walking to Caudale Moor with a return via a handy pub to Brothers Water.
Starting Point:	(GR 410130) Hartsop village off the A592, 2 miles south of Ullswater. Small car park.
Alternative Start:	(GR 402133) Cow Bridge on the A592. Car park.

The village of Hartsop was already in shadow and on the high fells the lingering patches of snow were beginning to turn orange. In the car park, boots and socks were being removed from tired feet; anoraks, woolly hats and gloves discarded, while rucksacks lay where they had fallen. At last the hills were empty. It was time to go up.

If you want to have the Lake District all to yourself, then timing is crucial and mid-winter summit camps are one of the finest ways possible, but the ascent of Hartsop Dodd never gets any easier and with rucksacks crammed with gear it was a very slow plod as we climbed away from the valley. Gradually the village grew smaller, the houses and the few remaining cars became toylike, while the view expanded to take in Brothers Water, Angletarn Pikes, and Ullswater. The last walker headed past us down the hill with his dog, but despite the late hour it still felt warm and it wasn't until the angle eased that we stopped to put on our windproofs.

With only just over a mile to the summit of Caudale Moor we gained height steadily, past snow piled in drifts against the wall, then, glancing down, we saw the figure of a man below us. He appeared to be in a hurry and as we watched he waved vigorously in our direction. We resumed our climb, but after fifteen minutes he had gained on us so much that we resolved to wait. By now we could see his dog, floundering through the snow in short bursts of energy only to subside again. The poor thing was doing its best, but it was obviously as puzzled as we were why its master should choose to set off again after a full day on the hills.

"Have you seen my anorak?" he called. "I must have dropped it and it's got my car keys in the pocket." We took his address and he pounded past up the hill. "Just time for a look on the summit" he called as we paused to watch the final moments of the sun as it sank in a blaze of fire to the west.

The top of Caudale Moor is flat. Lots of room and an excellent campsite, but apart from the tarn there isn't any water. Tempting though it was to lighten

Frost on the Atkinson Memorial

the load by pitching the tent, caution said "What if you can't find it again in the dark?", so we pressed on, over the summit and down the southern side to look for a spring.

As once again we climbed to the top, the cloud came in. Not the grey, blot-out-everything-and-get-you-wet sort of cloud, but a luminous silver mist that rolled silently up the slope beside us. Then, as we pitched the tent, the cloud vanished and we looked out on a starry moonlit world, not colourless, but blue-black, with a faint streak of orange still in the sky where the sun had so recently been.

It was rather early for dinner, so instead we went to look at the memorial cairn, but on the way back the cloud returned. One moment there was the black silhouette of the distant fells, the next only a faint luminescence about us and nothing to be seen. Slowly we walked across the flat, featureless, moorlike expanse to where the tent had been. Casting to left and right the light of our headtorches was little help in the enveloping mist until, moving carefully forward, we came to the wall. We had walked straight past the tent.

It was a quiet night, though towards dawn the wind seemed to have got up a bit, but a brief look through the stiff frozen folds of the doorway showed only patches of snow, hoar frost and a swirling grey fog. The rucksacks were much lighter when we emerged, as today we were wearing most of the contents, and though the temperature was well below freezing, in the wind it felt even colder and we were keen to be on our way. But the tent was beautiful. Every edge and seam, and every guyrope, had grown a plume, a feather of frost, and it was almost reluctantly that we packed the frozen tent into the sack, breaking the winter sculpture into slivers of ice.

ROUTE DESCRIPTION

Hartsop Dodd (*Stag valley round hill*)

From Hartsop village car park take the track across Walker Bridge, the packhorse bridge over Hayeswater Gill, then at the bend, head up the grass beside the wall to a stile. It is a remarkably unrelenting climb, continuing straight up to the ridge, and soon the village is beneath your feet. On the eastern flank of the fell are the remains of old lead mines, part of the Low Hartsop Mine whose workings can be seen in the valley below. Though the vein consisted mostly of quartz, work continued here, when the lower levels flooded, until the late 1880s.

As the skyline is reached there is a superb aerial view of Brothers Water, but with little respite the path continues at the same angle, following the nose of the fell, and zigzagging steeply upwards. At length a large cairn appears, and though it turns out to be no more than the end of a wall, it is only a little further to the summit cairn. The actual highest point of Hartsop Dodd (2028ft) is by the wall and just a few yards beyond. Looking back down to Patterdale Place Fell stands isolated beside Ullswater, while to the west rises the long high ridge of the Helvellyn Range.

Stony Cove Pike

Whatever the weather, navigation presents no problems, just follow the wall. With views down into the hidden valley of Caudale to the right, a gentle climb of little over a mile brings you to the top of Stony Cove Pike (2503ft), the summit of Caudale Moor, and away to the east is the 14ft high beacon on Thornthwaite Crag.

Caudale Moor Tarn (*Tarn on the moor above the valley of the calves*)

The summit tarn lies due west, and in mist the adjacent wall is a useful guide in the flat and featureless surroundings. Though rather dreary on dull days, any tarn of this size, when reflecting a brilliant blue sky, can be delightful.

A few yards to the south-west is a cairn topped with a wooden cross, a memorial to Mark Atkinson who bought the Kirkstone Inn in 1914, and also

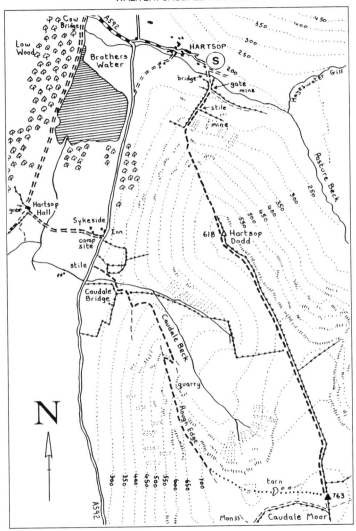

2.4

to his son William. From the cairn you can see the inn which at one time was claimed to be the highest in England. Further west the prominent cairn on the skyline is John Bell's Banner, named after the Rev John Bell, vicar of Ambleside in the sixteenth century, while the word 'Banner' refers to the parish boundary.

Brothers Water Inn

The descent lies to the north-west where a line of cairns sets off down Rough Edge, the superb north-west ridge of Caudale Moor. The path, which is rather indistinct, keeps to the crest to pass above a disused slate quarry before meeting an old track coming up from the right. Follow this down to the ruined quarry huts and spoil heaps, but do not enter any of the old workings which are unsafe. There are at least two adits entering the hillside, higher up in the main quarry is another tunnel, and on our last visit here we found an old bedstead and a shining new pound coin.

From the quarry a grooved path, an old sled gate, descends the ridge to reach the beck near Caudale Bridge, then crossing the stream below the rocky ravine, the road is joined for a short way to the Brothers Water Inn.

Brothers Water

From the inn the public footpath to Patterdale leads through Sykeside campsite to the 400-year-old Hartsop Hall. This replaced an earlier twelfth-century hall, built when the valley was part of a Norman hunting forest as shelter for the monks travelling from Furness Abbey to Lanercost Priory. It was given to the National Trust in 1946.

The track goes round the back of the hall and on beside Brothers Water, once called Broad Water but given its present name after two brothers were drowned here while skating in 1785. Low Wood, with its oak, ash and hazel, is classified as a Site of Special Scientific Interest and has changed little since Dorothy Wordsworth wrote "I left William sitting on the bridge, and went along the path on the right of the wood. I was delighted with what I saw:- the water under the bare old trees, the simplicity of the mountains, and the exquisite beauty of the path....I could have stayed for ever".

Hartsop (*Stag valley*)

Reaching the car park at Cow Bridge, turn right along the footpath beside the main road for about 300 yards and then go left down the lane into the picturesque Hartsop village. Said by Wordsworth to be a 'decaying hamlet' the cottages are now nearly all holiday homes. It is strange to think that this delightful little village was once the most important place in the Patterdale valley and the centre of a very busy industrial area with charcoal huts, potash kilns, watermills and of course the lead mines.

WALK 2.5: HAYESWATER, BROCK CRAGS & ANGLE TARN

Tarns:	Hayeswater
	Satura Crag Tarn
	Brock Crags Tarns
	Angle Tarn
Distance:	6½ miles
Ascent:	1300ft
Summary:	Mainly good fell paths lead to delightful tarns and a quiet summit.
Starting Point:	(GR 410130) Hartsop village, 2 miles south of Ullswater. Small car park.

No more than a tiny blue dot on the map, almost invisible without a magnifying glass, the diminutive tarn seemed destined to remain undiscovered, until stepping over the tumbled stone wall that hides it from

Satura Crag Tarn

61

view we found the lovely little rocky pool of Satura Crag. With its sapphire blue waters cupped among the rocks on the very edge of the fell, it looks steeply down to Hayeswater far below, across the valley is the long ridge of Grey Crag, and yet only yards away is the path to Angle Tarn.

Though lacking the drama of its namesake under the shadowed northern cliffs of Bow Fell, the Angle Tarn of the Far Eastern Fells is an altogether friendlier place, more open to the sky and more often catching the sunlight. Other tarns may have grander settings, but here, surrounded by low craggy summits, its coves, headlands, and little rocky island seem like a Lake District in miniature, a tarn in name but a lake in spirit.

We have spent many hours on the shores of Angle Tarn. One February night, with the tarn frozen inches thick, we listened to the ghostly sounds of the ice stretching and singing, and woke to a cloudless morning with hoarfrost crystals sparkling like diamonds. In spring at four o'clock in the morning we have heard the song of the lark, and in a summer heatwave we splashed in the cool water and swam to the little island.

Now swimming in tarns is more often planned than accomplished, for even on a scorching summer day the first tentative dip of a toe in the icy water is usually sufficient discouragement. But for the late Timothy Tyson and Colin Dodgson, collecting tarns was no mere toe-dipping affair. In 1959 these two hardy men from Grasmere decided to swim in every tarn in Lakeland. Starting with the well-known ones they soon began to search out those more remote, while even private tarns were included, visited under cover of darkness. They never bothered about swimsuits and amazingly never saw anyone; though whether anyone saw them is another matter. It took eight years, and when the task was declared complete, they had swum in over 450 tarns. Though rather more than we have found, perhaps when one has thrown oneself naked in mid-winter into ice-cold water on a fellside, it would seem churlish to say afterwards it wasn't really a tarn.

It was late in the afternoon as we came down to the edge of Angle Tarn. The sun still shone out of a cloudless blue sky, there was only the gentlest of breezes, the distant fells shimmered in the heat, and for once the idea of a swim seemed attractive.

While some advocate the sudden total immersion method, ours is the more cautious approach, but after several minutes during which feet, then legs, then thighs became reluctantly accustomed to the cold, we counted to three and ducked beneath the surface.

It was perfect; lazily we swam round in circles, then becoming more bold struck out towards the island. As we hauled ourselves out of the water onto the rocky heather covered knoll we noticed the new arrivals. Perhaps swimming in tarns is becoming more popular, perhaps even the exploits of the men from Grasmere are being emulated, for certainly the figure beside the water hadn't bothered about a costume, but it definitely wasn't a man.

Winter camp at Angle Tarn

ROUTE DESCRIPTION

Hayeswater (*Lake by the enclosure or Eithr's lake*)

From Hartsop the road goes through the car park, and past some large sheep pens, to continue as a bridleway to Hayeswater. Follow the tarmac up the valley, which has the classic glacial U-shape, and fork right on an unsurfaced track to cross Hayeswater Gill. Below, at the confluence of the main stream with Pasture Beck, are the remains of Low Hartsop Mine, which was worked for lead from 1867, but troubled with collapses and flooding, the mine was never a commercial success and had to be abandoned 20 years later. The two parallel walls once housed a water-wheel 30ft in diameter.

After crossing the gill the track climbs steeply uphill above the cascades, and on the far bank is the Filter House from which a pressure pipeline leads to Boredale Hause. Reaching the dam, Hayeswater appears ahead in its high valley, where frost-shattered rocks and hummocky glacial moraines of boulder clay look as though the Ice Age has only just come to an end. The reservoir supplies water to the local villages and also to Penrith.

Satura Crag Tarn (*Robber's crag tarn*)

Just below the dam a footbridge crosses Hayeswater Gill and the path heads straight up the grassy hillside to a rocky outcrop. To avoid unnecessary ascent, turn left across a small stream to a gap in the broken wall, then keeping above the intake wall, Sulphury Gill is crossed. The broad path is joined which contours round the lower slopes of Rest Dodd, whose name has nothing to do with relaxation, but probably means the rough round hill.

Following the fence with good views down to Hayeswater, the path then rounds a rocky knoll at the head of Bannerdale, the valley of the holly trees. There are several little boggy pools, but on the far side of the broken wall and at its highest point is a real gem of a tarn. This natural little rock pool on the very edge of the fell is in a superb position with a bird's-eye view of Hayeswater.

Brock Crags Tarns (*Tarns on the badger's cliffs*)

The path continues to a small gate, but must now be abandoned to visit the tarns of Brock Crags. Turning left, a narrow trod leads down beside the wall, and crossing an intervening wall in the dip, climbs again. Reaching the highest point, head due west straight for the summit cairn, where the twin tarns will be found in a hollow between the grassy knolls. It is now only a few extra feet to the summit of Brock Crags (1841ft) from which there are fine views of Hayeswater, Angle Tarn and Ullswater.

Angle Tarn (*Fishing tarn*)

Though pathless, it is now quite easy walking to Angle Tarn. Head north to join a wall and follow it down on the far side to the marsh, then after crossing

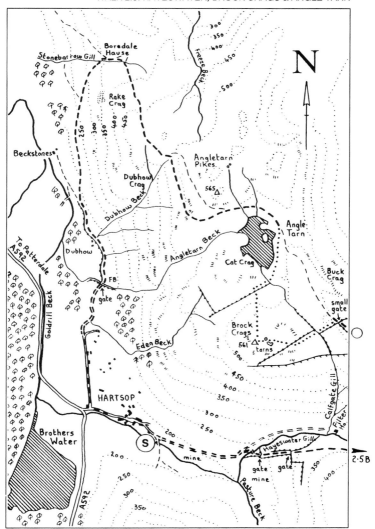

2.5A

a little stream, the grassy banks of Angle Tarn are reached. This is a beautiful spot with little bays to explore, an island, an inviting peninsula, and on one visit, a whole tribe of nude bathers.

Boredale Hause (*The pass of the valley with the barn*)

Rejoining the main path, it curves past Angletarn Pikes to become a delightful little alpine trod high above the valley, with Brothers Water, Deepdale and Patterdale far below. A less obvious path joins the route and you continue downhill to Boredale Hause where over to the right are the ruins of the medieval chapel. In the summer of 1805 an old man cutting peat sheltered here from a storm, and Wordsworth used this incident in his epic poem *The Excursion*.

Patterdale Valley (*St Patrick's valley*)

At the col, cross Stonebarrow Gill and follow it down for a short way before recrossing the stream. The path now heads straight for Brothers Water, and passing above Beckstones Farm on the line of the Hayeswater Pipeline, the

2.5B

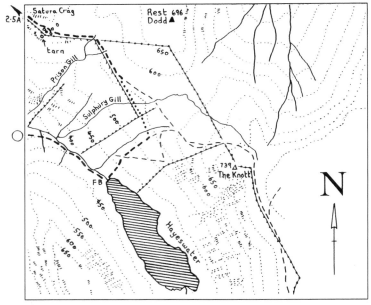

main path is joined in the valley.

Crossing the footbridge beneath the falls of Angletarn Beck, which can look very fine after rain, a rough and stony old road leads past the chalets at Hartsop Fold. The road then becomes metalled, and at the T-junction you go left into the hamlet which was originally known as Low Hartsop.

There are still many buildings dating from the seventeenth century and two galleries where the wool was spun by the women of the family and then hung out to dry. These spinning galleries, which were mostly sited to the north and east of the buildings, were also used as a storage area and gave access to the upper floors. There is an old barn, said to have been a kiln for drying grain in the sixteenth century, and there was once a busy trade with Ambleside in charcoal, wool and timber.

3: Haweswater Tarns

WALK 3.1: HIGH RAISE TO BAMPTON COMMON

Tarns:	Redcrag Tarn
	Four Stones Tarn
Distance:	10½ miles
Ascent:	2000ft
Summary:	Remote pathless grassy ridges climb from Haweswater to High Street. Easy fell walking, but difficult navigation in mist.
Starting Point:	(GR 508161) Burnbanks, at the foot of Haweswater Reservoir. Parking on verge.

The sudden bleat of a sheep, sounding so close, startled us. The empty moor stretched into the distance and there was nothing to be seen. Strange how sound carries, we thought, and turned to walk away, but then again came the unmistakable noise, insistent and somehow urgent. It must be hidden, maybe in a bog, we agreed, and began to quarter the ground carefully, yet not quite sure, because how could a sheep remain concealed on this short-cropped turf? There was simply nowhere to hide. But trapped it certainly was. A tuft of wool, a couple of horns, and two frightened eyes were all that remained above ground. The rest was submerged, sunk in the black mire that filled a narrow slot in the ground. We grabbed it by the horns and by its thick, slimy, matted wool and heaved. The sheep went limp. Again we heaved, and again, for wet sheep are incredibly heavy, but slowly, very slowly, it rose from its grave, until with a final effort we dragged the soggy mass onto solid ground. The sheep looked around. It stood up. It shook itself in a slightly irritated way, and then without a backward glance tottered off rather unsteadily towards the rest of the flock. We cleaned ourselves as best we could and resumed the walk to Redcrag Tarn.

Redcrag Tarn is a typical moorland pool, a hollow in the peat surrounded by rough, tussocky grass on the long broad ridge that stretches north from High Raise, Wainwright's "last true mountain of the range". The atmosphere is one that depends almost entirely on the weather; dull and characterless on grey or wet days, but a delightful smiling landscape under a blue sky. Continuing north to Wether Hill, where wild ponies may be seen and even deer, these fells are a long way from habitation and it is a good place to save for a Bank Holiday as few people seek out the solitude of Bampton Common above Haweswater.

Anne rescuing sheep

While other lakes, notably Thirlmere, have been appropriated by the waterboards, only Haweswater has been singled out by the Ordnance Survey to be named a reservoir. In times of drought its principal function cannot be ignored, but Haweswater is still an attractive lake and the ascent beside Measand Beck one of the delights of the Eastern Fells. The transformation of the lake, wrought by Manchester with the construction of a 120ft high dam, made it the longest reservoir in the north-west. When the valley was flooded, the old village of Mardale Green was destroyed and part of the stonework of the old church is incorporated into the new dam.

Few people indeed are seen on the slopes above Haweswater, but the lake's western shore is now traversed by a famous long distance path. This has become so popular that every year a friend of ours acts as a guide to parties of Americans following the Coast to Coast Walk. We once met him on the lakeside path, a surprise for us both, but his party were unimpressed: the Lake District is such a small place that of course their leader would know everyone.

ROUTE DESCRIPTION

Haweswater (*Hafr's lake*)

From the waterworks houses at Burnbanks, a signpost points to the fellside track along the north-west shore of Haweswater. The bungalows are soon left behind, and the track bends uphill to a wooden step stile by a gate. One expects the high concrete dam retaining Haweswater Reservoir to dominate the scene, but it is hidden among the trees, and walking past the wood, ahead you can see the route up the grassy prow of Measand End. In the distance at the head of the lake is the craggy face of Harter Fell, to the right a fine cairn stands on the shoulder of Four Stones Hill, and in summer the grassy banks of the lake are covered with the purple spires of foxgloves.

On the far shore the steep wooded slopes of the Naddle Forest, an ancient oakwood, rise above the Haweswater Hotel. This is a modern replacement for the old Dun Bull Inn, demolished in 1936, while the only sign of the vanished village of Mardale Green are the windows from the church which have been incorporated into the little reservoir tower.

Low Raise (*Low cairn*)

After crossing the bridge over Measand Beck, leave the lakeside path and climb to the left of the stream. Little waterfalls, a narrow gorge with silver water dashing down over the rocks, and a natural garden of purple heather and golden tormentil, make this a delightful spot. Before the valley was flooded by Manchester Corporation, Measand Hall stood near here and also the village school which was founded in 1711.

Reaching a footbridge, a narrow trod sets off up the hill towards Measand End, then an old grooved path, now boggy and full of golden lesser spearwort, slants right and zigzags up the hill. Below is the flat expanse of Fordingdale Bottom, a hanging valley which looks as though it once held a tarn.

As the path peters out, continue climbing up the nose of the fell, heading south-west over the short, pathless grass. The angle eases as you reach some peat hags, and by a prominent isolated peaty knoll the summits of Low Raise and High Raise appear ahead. From the shores of Haweswater to the summit of Low Raise there is not a single cairn, which must be a record for the Lake District. Continue along the ridge, following sheep trods, or rather pony trods, and keeping over to the left there is a splendid view down into Whelter Bottom where we saw three deer and a group of black fell ponies with a foal.

A path develops as you near the summit of Low Raise, and from the pointed cairn, fashioned from an ancient tumulus, you can look back down the long grassy ridge, or across the Eden valley towards the Cross Fell Range, where sunlight highlights the radar dome on Great Dun Fell.

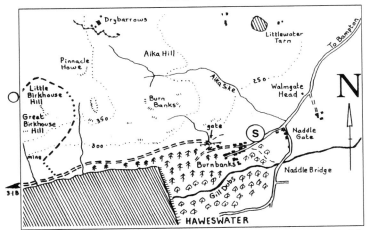

3.1A

High Raise (*High cairn*)

After the trackless sea of grass on the approach, all feet now head the same way, creating a path which follows the ridge to High Raise. The views are distant ones, but many of the giants of Lakeland are to be seen. To the west stretches the long Helvellyn Range, where the pointed summit of Catstye Cam is a marker for identifying the other tops, and beyond the dip of Grisedale Tarn is the characteristic shape of Great Gable, while to the north-west lies Skiddaw, with its neighbour Blencathra streaked by gullies on the southern face.

After an easy stroll there is a final pull up to the short turf of High Raise summit (2631ft), which is dominated by a large pile of stones beside the windbreak. From here Ullswater looks like two separate lakes lying at different levels, while to the north Redcrag Tarn can be seen shining on the grassy ridge, sandwiched between the wall and fence.

Redcrag Tarn

Joining the main path, which for some strange reason avoids the summit, head north along the broad ridge. To the left is the deep valley of Ramps Gill, which was used as a firing range during the war. The red roofed Bungalow, once a Victorian hunting lodge, was where the officers were housed. There are no public footpaths in the valley for on the far side of the meandering beck stands the Nab, which is a deer sanctuary and part of the Martindale Deer Forest.

71

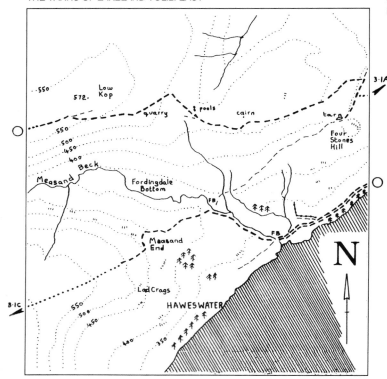

3.1B

A ruined fence and wall march in tandem along the top, but when they diverge, follow the fence which leads to the little peat moss tarn. Redcrag Tarn is just to the right of the path, but few walkers step aside to admire it, even though this is the only significant stretch of water in over 8 miles on the high-level ridge between Kentmere and the final 2000ft top of Loadpot Hill.

Four Stones Tarn

The main path, which is the line of the old Roman road from Ambleside to Penrith, continues over the grassy top of Red Crag, marked by a cairn just to the left of the fence, and then descends to Keasgill Head. There are fine views of Ullswater, which appears to be divided in two by Hallin Fell, while

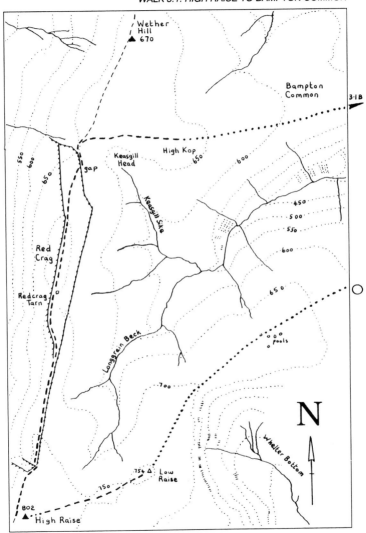

3.1C

beyond are the outlying conical hills of Great Mell Fell and Little Mell Fell. These isolated hills rising steeply from the plain are a hard conglomerate made of assorted fragments of many different Lakeland rocks welded together.

After crossing to the other side of the wall, which soon turns away downhill, the path continues along the ridge towards Wether Hill, but after 75 yards, at a small cairn, take the indistinct grassy trod forking right. It is easy walking, though soon there is little sign of a path across this moor-like hill, and only a solitary boundary stone, bearing the letter L, marks the summit of High Kop and the edge of the Lowther estate. Lowther Castle is near Penrith, but the grand mansion is now a shell and the grounds are a Wildlife Country Park.

Continuing east along the broad grassy ridge of Bampton Common, Haweswater comes into view. The indistinct path stays on the high moor, but gradually approaches the edge, where you look down into the valley of Measand Beck. Nearing the slight rise of Low Kop the path forks and, becoming more definite, begins to descend. Soon an old slate quarry is reached. After going through a little cutting, the grooved, rush-filled quarry track bends back to pass two small pools, then curving round the hill ahead, which is marked by a fine pointed cairn, continues along the fellside.

As the tarn comes into view beneath Four Stones Hill, continue down the track to an obvious junction where you turn right. Close by the tarn, which tends to dry up in summer, is an ancient cairn topped by a stone-walled enclosure, and beyond the tarn two standing stones frame a grand view of Haweswater.

Haweswater

From Four Stones Tarn head back along the path, and then turn off north-east to follow the shallow valley which runs below the main path round the slopes of Little Birkhouse Hill. Soon a grassy trod materialises which skirts the bog, heading south past Pinnacle Howe. Following the valley down there is a network of ways through the dense bracken, awkward to negotiate in summer, but slanting right a good path leads down to copper mine spoil heaps where there are three old levels, one containing a 55ft deep shaft. It is then an easy descent to the lakeside path which is followed back to Burnbanks where many of the bungalows are now lived in by the reservoir staff.

WALK 3.2: HIGH STREET

Tarns:	Blea Water
	Caspel Gate Tarn
	Small Water
Distance:	5 miles
Ascent:	1950ft
Summary:	Two magnificent corrie tarns linked by an ascent of High Street.
Starting Point:	(GR 469107) The head of Haweswater. Small car park.

"There is another Britain, to many of us the better half, a land of mountains and moorlands and of sun and cloud." These might be the words of a poet, and perhaps in a sense they are, for Professor Pearsall in his classic volume *Mountains and Moorlands* was always aware of the fragile beauty of the things he studied. His book is one of the finest attempts ever made to bridge the gap between the scientist and the amateur, that lover of wild places who just wants to know more about the hills.

There was to have been a sequel. For several years Professor Pearsall had been putting together notes for a new book with the Lake District as its exclusive subject, but dissatisfied with his early efforts he destroyed his half-finished manuscript, and then with tragic suddenness he died. Could anything be saved? All that remained were his notes and the overall plan for the book, but in 1973, some nine years after his death, the results of his work were published. It had been a massive effort, by both friends and colleagues, but principally by Dr Winifred Pennington.

The Lake District is a deceptively simple title. How many books have been published before with such a grand subject! How few have lived up to their aims! But this one is different. It tells you why the starry saxifrage grows among the rocks of the Scafells, and about the mosses that colonise the bare summits. It explains why there are stone stripes on Skiddaw, and how, as other tarns vanished, Small Water and Blea Water came to survive high in their ice-sculpted combes.

Blea Water, one of the deepest of the Lakeland tarns, lies in a steep sided hollow high on the eastern slopes of High Street. Here, over the million years that we call the Ice Age, the snows accumulated layer upon layer and turned slowly to ice. As the ice became a glacier and began to flow inexorably downhill, rocks trapped by the ice ground away a hollow and built a pile of debris on the lip. This happened in many such places, usually on eastern slopes where snow was heaviest on the lee side of the mountain. When the Ice Age came to an end, many of these upland hollows became tarns, but then the becks began to flow and as they did the running water started to nibble away at the retaining mounds of loose rock. This loose material was only a temporary barrier which soon gave way, and then, with a rush, the tarns emptied themselves down the mountainsides.

Well, why didn't this happen to all the tarns? The answer for Small Water is that the beck moved. For some reason the original outlet became blocked, the stream was diverted and began to spill over a barrier of solid rock. And it is the rock barrier that has preserved this delightful tarn. Once it was thought this was the reason for all the surviving corrie tarns, but for Blea Water the story is different. The massive high wall of moraine has been cut through by the stream, yet the tarn lives on, for here the glacier carved a deep hollow in the rock, and the tarn lies in a basin over 200ft deep.

Not only has Blea Water survived, its surroundings are unusual too. The mountains of the Lakes have relatively few flowers because the acid soil lacks the lime needed to sustain a variety of plant life. Yet the rocks of central Lakeland are not inherently poor, it is just that after ten thousand years of rain the free lime has been washed away. But the rocks above Blea Water are exceptionally rich in calcium, and on the cliffs, well out of the reach of the sheep, rare arctic-alpine plants can be found.

Botanists are hardy creatures, scrambling into inaccessible places on the fells, and in their hands many of them will be clutching a book. The botanist's bible, the small but substantial volume consulted by many an expert crouching over some new discovery, is *A Field Excursion Flora* by Clapham, Tutin and Warburg, or *CTW* as it is affectionately known. The name Tutin seemed familiar, now where had we seen that before? *The Lake District* gave us the answer, for it's on the title page. Under "Dr Winifred Pennington" is her married name, "Mrs T.G. Tutin". It's a small world.

John backpacking

ROUTE DESCRIPTION

Blea Water (*Dark blue lake*)

Leaving the car park at the end of Haweswater an old road continues over the Gatescarth Pass, but after 50 yards you turn right along the lake shore. Before the reservoir was constructed in 1935, the village of Mardale Green stood at the head of the valley.

After crossing Mardale Beck turn up beside it to a ladder stile and then climb by the pretty falls of Dodderwick Force. The confluence of Small Water Beck and Blea Water Beck is reached, and the path continues over another ladder stile beside more attractive waterfalls, gaining height steadily to pass a disused slate quarry on the far side of the stream. Immediately after the Ice Age a tarn filled this boggy hollow and you can see how the beck cut down through the glacial moraine. Most of the glacial moraines to be seen in the Lake District were left by the final glaciation, for each successive advance of the ice swept away all traces of former glaciers, but high on Caspel Gate the mounds are said to be remnants of even older times.

The path becomes rather faint, but keeping uphill out of the boggy area, it eventually reappears and climbs beside the beck to join a higher path just before Blea Water is reached. The ugly concrete dam, a reminder that it is still used as a reservoir, whose water is piped to Swindale to supply local villages, is a poor introduction to Blea Water, for this is a beautiful mountain tarn. The deepest in the Lake District, it has a wild and dramatic setting in a perfect corrie formed by the crags of High Street.

Caspel Gate Tarn

The path, which at first is rather indistinct, turns uphill at the dam to climb the steep grassy slope. Just before the ridge is gained, turn right past some obvious white quartz rocks to reach Caspel Gate. The pretty little tarn, though barely more than a large peaty pool perched on the grassy col, is in a delightful position. Although quite shallow, it seems to resist all but prolonged drought.

To the north, across the valley of Riggindale, Kidsty Pike, the goat's path peak, looks a fine summit, but it is the nearer crags of this valley that have been the focus of interest, for since the 1970s Golden Eagles have nested here. Riggindale is now an RSPB (Royal Society for the Protection of Birds) reserve, and in 1992 when a chick was raised to adulthood, the RSPB publicised the attraction and over 10,000 people visited the hide.

High Street (*High upland pasture*)

The ridge, which links Rough Crag with High Street, is the best of all possible ways to the summit, and following the good path which climbs westwards along the airy crest, it is over all too soon and you emerge at the cairn on the edge of the grassy top.

Blea Water now appears almost vertically below, the full length of

Haweswater Reservoir can be seen, and 20 miles away to the north-east is Cross Fell. Aim south-west to join the wall which traverses the fell and this brings you to High Street's concrete OS trig point at 2717ft. The summit is so flat that you can see only the tops of the surrounding fells, though there is a good view of Fairfield and Helvellyn to the west, while above Dove Crag lie the unmistakable shapes of Great Gable and the Scafells.

The name High Street refers to the Roman road from Galava to Brocavum near Penrith, which runs a little way below the summit on the western side, though the route was almost certainly in use as far back as Neolithic times. The mountain was also known as Racecourse Hill for a shepherds' fair was held here in July, when fell ponies were raced over the tops. The celebrations, the last one being in 1835, lasted for several days. There were wrestling matches, trials of strength, various games and sports, and as well as large quantities of food, beer was brought up by the barrel. Our refreshment was more sober, though, when we camped on the summit as the stream that tumbles over the crag supplies only water.

Small Water

The wall continues southwards towards the distant twin cairned summit of Ill Bell and away to the right lies the prominent column of Thornthwaite Beacon. After about 350 yards, with Windermere in sight ahead, fork left at a small cairn on a little path which initially goes south-east, then bends left before resuming its course to Mardale Ill Bell. The summit lies on the far side of an area of rocky knolls, and though with so little rise it fails to qualify as a separate mountain, a magnetic attraction always lures us to the cairn.

The path continues downhill and soon Small Water comes into view far below. Descending now more steeply, the tall wall shelter at the top of the Nan Bield Pass is reached. Harriet Martineau wrote of coming this way in 1854 in her *Guide to the Lakes*, and the pass was in regular use as early as 1533, linking Kendal with Penrith, predating the more modern route over Shap. To the south-west lies Kentmere Reservoir, a large artificial stretch of water beneath the switchback ridge of Yoke, Ill Bell and Froswick, but turning the opposite way, the path zigzags steeply down the old packhorse way to Small Water, 600ft below. This is "the finest of Lakeland's tarns", says Wainwright, and few would disagree.

When the tarn is reached there are three stone-roofed shelters beside the path, an indication of how busy this route must once have been, though one would have to be hard pressed to squeeze into them now. The bridleway follows the water's edge, with steep slopes falling to the shoreline, and on the col to the north is a large shallow pool. Crossing the outflow of the tarn, the path follows Small Water Beck down beside its waterfalls, and back to the end of Haweswater Reservoir, where sadly the Dun Bull Inn is no more and the nearest hostelry is now the Haweswater Hotel, built by Manchester Corporation very inconveniently halfway down the lake.

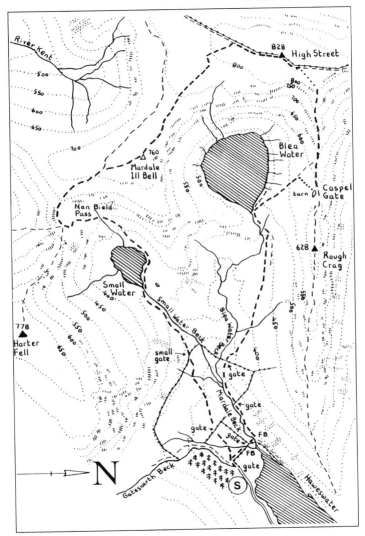

3.2

WALK 3.3: BRANSTREE AND SWINDALE

Tarns:	Branstree Tarn
	Howes Tarn
Distance:	7¹/₂ miles
Ascent:	2350ft
Summary:	Unfrequented fells on the eastern fringe of the Lakes where deer are more often seen than walkers.
Starting Point:	(GR 469107) The head of Haweswater Reservoir. Car park.

High above Haweswater, on the grassy col between Branstree and its north-eastern summit, stands a massive column of stone. After a lapse of 60 years it is beginning to show its age, but the engineers who constructed the Haweswater Reservoir built their surveying pillars solidly and well.

There have been many times when one of these would have come in handy, as once we too were surveyors. When we were writing *The Mountains of England and Wales*, which describes all the summits over 2000ft, sometimes the OS maps lacked detail and we did our own personal survey. It took two years, tramping the fells in all weathers and seasons, to establish the total of 432 tops, and standing beside Branstree's pillar as the cloud settled onto the fells, we sympathised with the waterboard surveyors who must often, like us, have been frustrated as the mist rolled in to obscure the view.

Though Thirlmere had been enlarged towards the end of the nineteenth century, Manchester and the growing population of the industrial north-west had an ever increasing need for water. By the early 1930s there was no longer enough, and Haweswater, the most easterly of the lakes, was chosen to supplement the supply, and a mile long dam was constructed. This nearly doubled the length of the lake to 4 miles, flooding the valley and drowning the picturesque village of Mardale Green.

The water from Thirlmere was piped direct to Manchester, flowing entirely by gravity along a 96 mile aqueduct, and Haweswater was to be linked with this by digging a 5 mile long tunnel under the hillside of the Naddle Forest to Longsleddale. In order to build the tunnel the surveyors erected two towers, one on Branstree and the other on the far side of Mosedale. Each was surrounded by a high wooden platform, level with the central notch, on which the engineers could stand. The surveying column is a little below the highest point of the col, but from the platform the surveyors would have been able to see both the head of the lake and the top of the Tarn Crag tower to the south. After the work was completed, the workmen gone and the valley, though flooded, peaceful once more, the towers were abandoned and left to crumble into ruins.

In 1978 another pipeline was built to join the lake to the thirsty south. This time the water flowed via Shap and was augmented by supplies diverted from Swindale. But this valley, once also earmarked for a reservoir, has remained unspoilt, while above it Mosedale lies deserted and remote, the haunt of the deer.

There was no surveying on this trip though. Our task was easier; all we had to decide was whether the nameless pool on Branstree's grassy col deserved its status as a tarn. As we tramped over the summit, and past the gaunt and windswept ruined tower, on the distant ridge we could just make out across the valley its companion silhouetted on Tarn Crag. Of course we would include Branstree Tarn. With such an eventful history, how could we leave it out?

ROUTE DESCRIPTION

Branstree (*Steep road*)

At the head of Haweswater a signpost points the way to the Gatescarth Pass and Longsleddale. Keeping to the main path, which in 1750 was referred to as the high road to Ambleside, it is a steady climb past the plantation. Ahead rise the steep crags of Harter Fell where a pair of Golden Eagles nested in

The survey pillar

the 1960s before moving house to the nearby valley of Riggindale.

Following the attractive waterfalls of Gatescarth Beck, the track ascends steadily to a sheepfold, where there is a momentary easing, before climbing on with renewed vigour. On reaching the top of the pass, and when the fence comes into view ahead, leave the old road to head left across pathless grass up the steep slopes of Branstree. There is a bit of a path beside the fence and the views south into Longsleddale are a good excuse for a pause in the climb.

Near the top of the fell is a boundary stone inscribed L for the Lowther estate, which belonged to Lord Lonsdale. A wall then comes up to join the fence, and the highest point of Branstree at 2339ft lies a few yards to the left, marked not by a trig point but by a concrete ring. The summit does not have much to recommend it as a viewpoint, but if you look between Harter Fell and Thornthwaite Beacon you can see the distant Scafells.

Branstree Tarn

From the OS marker a little grassy trod leads north-east, parallel to the fence, to the prominent cairn on Artle Crag. Here the rocks are set on end and stick up out of the ground like *chevaux de frise*. The fine stone man is much the best viewpoint, with Haweswater Reservoir set against a backdrop of the long High Street ridge. To the north-east the ancient cairn on the summit of Selside Pike stands out very clearly and beyond the ruined tower on the col, which separates Branstree from its subsidiary top, lies Branstree Tarn.

Returning to the fence, cross to the far side and descend the pathless grass to the stone pillar, which was built by the Haweswater surveyors during the construction of the Longsleddale aqueduct. The first water from the reservoir reached Manchester by this route in 1941. This surveying tower lines up with a similar structure on the summit of Tarn Crag which can be seen on the skyline to the south. A little to the east lies the first objective of the walk, Branstree Tarn. This peat moss tarn, which shares the col with an adjacent pool, has no little beaches, and the surrounding grassy moor stops abruptly at the edge of the dark water.

Howes Tarn (*Tarn on the hill*)

From the tarn head east over Branstree North East Top, where a few stones scraped together mark the highest point at 2208ft. Continuing east across pathless grass, in the distance is the Shap Granite Quarry, while to the left lurks the strangely named Captain Whelter Bog, named after a farm in the Mardale valley. Here we found a small upright stone, a 1911 memorial with later inscriptions, including one added in 1989 to the 'Deer Man'. This secluded fellside is a haven for deer and we have seen them on each of our visits, the last being a record for we counted 16 hinds.

Continue down the ridge, across a flat peaty area and over the rightmost rocky knoll to a grassy shelf. Howes Tarn is set on the far side of the outcrops

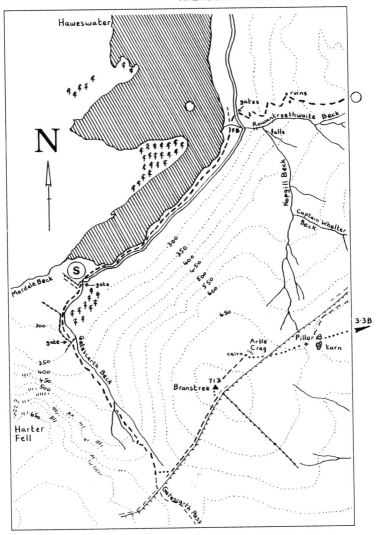

3.3A

and, like the one on Branstree, is a peat moss tarn, but with a far more attractive setting right on the edge of the fell. Grassy borders fringe the shallow water and from it you look across the empty valley of Mosedale to the cairn on the summit of Harrop Pike and down upon Mosedale Cottage. The disused Mosedale Quarry was started in the 1880s and despite its remote location was very prosperous. The stone was taken by cart to the terminus of the Lancaster Canal at Kendal, but by the end of the 1920s the quarry had ceased production.

Swindale (*Pig valley*)

Descending the pathless slopes into Mosedale, head eastwards towards the bridge over the stream, just below the confluence of Mosedale Beck and Little Mosedale Beck. The right of way, which runs along the valley above a ruined wall, is an old drove road. Indistinct at first, the rather boggy track passes under Ash Knot and past a couple of sheepfolds to a gate, and from here the ensuing walk down into Swindale is delightful. Among the gravel of the springs that edge the path the yellow mountain saxifrage can be found, while to the right Mosedale Beck tumbles down a series of rocky waterfalls. Mosedale is a hanging valley left behind as the Swindale glacier carved ever deeper, and there is much evidence of glacial action with heaps of terminal moraine through which the path threads its way.

As the valley floor is reached, the path follows a raised embankment carved by the ice between the river and Dodd Bottom, which must surely have once held a tarn. Nearby is Simon's Stone, a large isolated boulder left by the retreating ice and almost obscured by the surrounding trees. Becoming enclosed by walls, the track continues to the single remaining farm at Swindale Head, where on our last visit the hay in the fields was being turned by hand. At one time this valley too was considered for a reservoir, but though it was spared and the water extracted painlessly through a tunnel to Haweswater, the youth hostel is no more and, like Mardale, its school and church have been demolished. Stephen Walker, Swindale's vicar in the 1830s. was an enterprising man, for when he found the communion wine bottle had been broken, he used rum instead!

Old Corpse Road

At the farm go left through a field gate onto the Old Corpse Road, the route by which coffins were carried from Mardale to Shap parish church before the graveyard at Mardale was consecrated in 1729. When the reservoir was constructed and the church demolished, the bodies were exhumed and reburied at Shap with their ancestors.

The grassy track climbs steeply then crosses and recrosses the stream to reach the grassy moor. Continuing south-west by a reedy channel, the northern ridge of Selside Pike rises to the left and the track, now little more

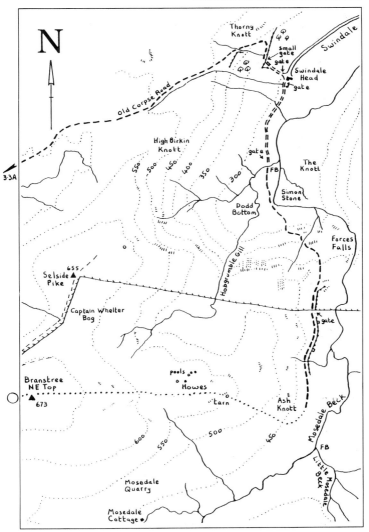

3.3B

than a narrow trod, wanders on across the moor. Gradually it starts to descend, and reaching a rocky knoll there is a ruined hut and another a little below, where peat was stored and dried before being used as fuel. The old road then zigzags down the hillside with the magnificent ravine of Rowantreethwaite Beck to the left, and steeply below is Haweswater Reservoir.

Reaching the road it is a mile back to the head of the lake, but to avoid the tarmac, go through the small gate opposite and take the little path along the lake shore. This leads down through the bracken and across a pretty stone footbridge, then on beside the reservoir, past the site of the drowned village of Mardale Green, and through a series of gaps in the walls, all the way back to the car park

WALK 3.4: WET SLEDDALE

Tarns:	Wet Sleddale Reservoir
	Haskew Tarn
Distance:	6¹/₂ miles
Ascent:	950ft
	(The short-cut by Sleddale Hall makes it 1 mile less)
Summary:	Easy walking over the quiet Shap Fells.
Starting Point:	(GR 555115) Wet Sleddale. Parking by the dam.

It was late in the afternoon as we climbed towards Haskew Tarn. The sun had disappeared behind the clouds, and rain was on its way again, but with any luck our tent would be pitched before it came. In the distance rose the white plumes of steam from the chimneys at Shap, but in the wild sweep of moorland there was no-one to be seen. We hadn't met anyone since breakfast above Kentmere and all day we had walked alone, for the Shap Fells, more reminiscent of the Pennines than the Lakes, are the quietest hills of all.

We were on a backpacking trip of discovery and this was new country, visited only once or twice on fleeting expeditions from the west to pick off the few tops that pushed their way through the 2000ft barrier. But we wanted to get to know the area better, to visit not only the handful of named tarns, but also those mysterious patches of blue that might be undiscovered gems. The best way of getting to know a place is to live in it for a while, so as the first few drops of rain fell, we pitched our tent beside the stream and made our home for the night.

It was nearly two years before we returned, and this time we approached from the east, turning off the motorway at Shap. The transition is sudden. One moment you are hemmed in by lorries and cars desperate to be somewhere else as fast as possible, the next you are on a deserted road. Within minutes we were parking our car by the dam of Wet Sleddale Reservoir where only one other vehicle, solitary and empty, stood at the road end.

Wainwright's map looked strangely out of scale until we realised that the reservoir has grown and the water now laps closer to the barn at New Ings. We strolled along the track and down to the footbridge which looks quite at home across Sleddale Beck, though it is an "off-comer", rebuilt here when its original home disappeared beneath the water. Then climbing past Sleddale Hall we reached the open moor.

Nothing here had changed. A pair of lapwings tumbled in the air, their wild cries the only sound save for the song of a skylark, a tiny speck high above. In the valley below stood the high walls of an ancient deer enclosure and in the distance was the hazy blue outline of High Street. Ahead of us Haskew Tarn lay in its peaty hollow and in the sunlight the grass gleamed silver-gold.

It was an easy walk back down the valley, a gentle path high above Sleddale Beck, the hills seeming even quieter than usual with the sheep down in the fields for lambing. At Green Farm a tractor chugged slowly up the lane. Then we were back. Beside the solitary car there now stood another. It was a secret assignation; a handover, for after a brief chat the first car drove off down the lane, while the new arrival, a tall man with a far-away look in his eyes and a pair of binoculars, set off up the fellside.

Sleddale Hall

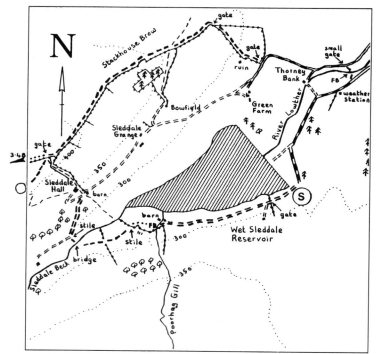

3.4A

ROUTE DESCRIPTION

Sleddale Hall (*Sleddale is a tautology as both sled and dale mean valley*)
Leaving the end of the dam, a bridleway leads through a gate and along the hillside above Wet Sleddale Reservoir. The reservoir, which obliterated all traces of the valley's former common field, was built to supplement Haweswater, and has a capacity of 500 million gallons. Forking right to New Ings, go to the left of the old barn where the footpath crosses Poorhag Gill by a little footbridge, and the wall is surmounted by a ladder stile.

The public right of way now descends to cross Sleddale Beck at the stepping stones, but if the beck is too deep to cross, it is easier to go to the left of the knoll and follow the white topped posts which mark the line of the bridleway to the little packhorse bridge. This was moved from its original site when the reservoir was made in the early 1960s and was reconstructed by

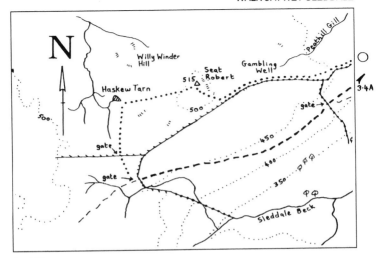

3.4B

Manchester Corporation. Beyond the bridge is a stile and then climbing to join a track you turn right to the seventeenth-century Sleddale Hall.

Seat Robert (*Robert's upland pasture*)

Past the hall a footpath squeezes between the stream and the wall and climbs to a barred footbridge. Just beyond there is a pretty waterfall and a little pool, and the path continues climbing beside the stream to reach a ladder stile over the top wall. A faint track on the far side follows this wall, cutting across the bleak grassy moorland when it bends away, and soon Seat Robert comes into view. Staying by the wall, which lapses momentarily into a fence, skirt Gambling Well, which is no more than a large bog, and at its highest point, when the wall again becomes a fence, turn uphill to climb to the top of Seat Robert (1690ft). A concrete ring marks the Ordnance Survey Trig Station, but the stones are somewhat older, being the remains of a large Bronze Age burial cairn. Beyond the steaming chimneys of the Shap Works and the busy M6 lies the Cross Fell Range, while to the south-east are the Howgills. Haskew Tarn is now in sight, and far beyond it to the right is the little point of Kidsty Pike and High Street.

Haskew Tarn

Heading just south of west, keep to the high ground and skirt the boggy pools

89

to reach Haskew Tarn. Sited by a rocky knoll its attraction lies in its isolation and depends on the weather and the season, but in summer with the pink flowers of bogbean growing among the reeds and water horsetail, it is pretty enough to please the most critical tarn bagger.

Wet Sleddale (*Wet valley*)

From the tarn a short climb southwards brings you to a gate which allows passage through the fence, and a little way downhill the bridleway from Longsleddale is joined. Once a very important highway, this former drove road led past the large slate quarry in the remote Mosedale which was worked from the 1800s.

Turn left over the ladder stile by a gate to follow the old track along the hillside high above the stream, which has cut down deeply to form a narrow ravine. On the far side of Sleddale Beck, you can see walls which were built long ago to trap deer. After about a mile, at another stile by a gate, the walk can be cut short by taking the zigzag track down to Sleddale Hall and then back past the reservoir along the outward route.

Continuing instead along the grassy track to the ladder stile which was crossed earlier, the bridleway follows the left side of the wall, and in the far distance is the flat summit of Cross Fell. The old way has deteriorated into a bog, but keeping by the wall a path descends Stackhouse Brow past a plantation to a gate. Just a mile away to the east is Shap Quarry, whose pink granite may be seen in Piccadilly Circus and St Paul's Cathedral.

As the old road bends round the wall and by the square ruin of Dale End, there is an unusual twin horse trough, and then the metalled lane from Green Farm is joined. Follow the road past the buildings at Thorney Bank to the footbridge over the River Lowther, and the tarmac road leads back past a weather station to the huge concrete reservoir dam.

4: Wythburn Tarns

WALK 4.1: HARROP TARN TO LAUNCHY TARN

Tarns:	Harrop Tarn
	Standing Crag Tarns
	Bell Crags Tarn
	Launchy Tarn
Distance:	4^{1}/$_{2}$ miles
Ascent:	1450ft
Summary:	Quiet, pathless fell walking above the forest. Not recommended in mist, can be boggy.
Starting Point:	(GR 316140) Dob Gill car park, on the west of Thirlmere. Toilets.

William Gilpin was much impressed. He had seen a wild-cat, and heard that the creature, "which Mr Pennant calls the British tyger", frequented the Thirlmere woods. But that was 1772, and very different from the Thirlmere of today. The woods were oak and ash, hazel, birch and sycamore, and the lake was two almost separate meres, joined at a shallow waist and crossed by stone piers linked by wooden bridges. There was the village of Wythburn, the Cherry Tree Inn, and Armboth House, where ghosts were said to hold an annual feast. This was the valley known by the Lake Poets, but a little over a hundred years later all was to change as Manchester Corporation, after defeating the conservationists, built their new reservoir and began to clothe the valley sides with conifers. "The lake and its surroundings are to be converted into an extensive people's park", complained Mr Howard, MP for East Cumberland who, like many of the protesters, wanted Thirlmere left "small, wild and inaccessible".

But although Thirlmere and its bare slopes were transformed, the lake remained inaccessible, for to protect the purity of their investment, the waterboard insisted that the shore was barred to all. They had promised to plant native trees, but ignored this undertaking, which surprisingly was overlooked until 1985 when they were forced to answer in court, and it was only with the building of an underground treatment works that Thirlmere was opened up to the general public. Now a attractive footpath follows the lake shore and Harrop Tarn is the objective of many a family walk climbing beside the waterfalls through the mature pines of the forest.

The figure coming down the hillside seemed to be in a hurry and, although carrying a massive bulging rucksack, soon caught up with us. "Did

Harrop Tarn

you see me land?" he asked eagerly, still panting with the effort of running. "I'm lucky to find you" he added, "I need someone to sign my log." And yes, we had seen him, flying overhead, a small figure beneath his huge multi-coloured parachute canopy. He had taken off that morning from Coniston Old Man, just above the quarries, and then, finding a good thermal, had soared over Wetherlam, Lingmoor Fell, and high across Langdale, where far below the black-headed gulls swarmed and squabbled over Youdell Tarn. Then on he went, over High Raise and Ullscarf until, as a thin veil of cloud came in from the west and the thermals began to die, he had picked a strip of open fellside and dropped to the ground nearly at our feet, just before the sea of conifers that swathe the slopes above Thirlmere. In his hand he carried what appeared to be a small handbag. "It's lead weights" he explained, "the canopy flies best with a heavier person and they're needed for ballast."

We walked back to our car where he dug in his pocket, saying "I'll show you where I've been". Producing a slim box about half the size of a paper-back book, he switched it on. "This tells me whether I'm going up or down" he said and thrusting the box suddenly above his head it gave a squeal which immediately changed to a lower tone as he brought it smartly down again. Once more he pressed the buttons and a screen lit up showing a picture of his flight over the Lake District fells, the ascents and descents, all plotted in a delicate silver graph.

ROUTE DESCRIPTION

Harrop Tarn (*Hares valley tarn*)

Leaving Dob Gill car park the footpath to Harrop Tarn goes up the steps and through a very tall kissing gate designed to keep out the deer. Then accompanied by the sound of waterfalls, which Coleridge on his way to Keswick in 1802 thought "the loudest in the whole country", the neatly made path zigzags uphill through the trees.

Surrounded by conifers, and dammed by glacial moraine, Harrop Tarn lies in a hollow beneath the huge cliffs of Tarn Crags, and though it is gradually silting up, the tarn is deep enough for fishing, which is free.

Standing Crag Tarns

Turn right on the forest road which passes the tarn to ford a stream by a footbridge, and keep straight ahead at the bend to take the bridleway, an ancient route to Watendlath. After briefly joining another forest road, the track, which is the higher, narrow path, climbs to the edge of the forest where a very grand double gate, constructed for horse riders, leads through the deer fence.

The path continues climbing to reach the fence on the rather boggy ridge, where you go through the kissing gate and ahead lies Blea Tarn, which is described in Volume 1. A short way to the left a pool straddles the fence and by it, under the rocky cliff of Standing Crag, are two sizeable peat bog tarns. The furthest, and largest, with an overhanging margin of moss, is deep enough for a swim, and both make an attractive foreground for the extensive panorama of the fells. To the east is Helvellyn, the high hills on the skyline to the north-west are the Grizedale Pike Range, in the northern distance you can see the Skiddaw Fells, while in the foreground is that favourite of every Keswick visitor, the ridge of Catbells.

Bell Crags Tarn

Returning to the kissing gate head north-east, aiming just to the right of a rocky knoll. The first gleam of water is only a small pool which dries up in the summer, but a few yards to the east, on the far side of the upthrust rocks, is a long narrow tarn set beneath a rocky cliff. It is a delightful spot, where we have yet to meet anyone else.

Launchy Tarn

After a brief climb north-west to a miniature summit at 1831ft, the highest point of Bell Crags, head north along the ridge and down to a high walled enclosure by a disused slate quarry. This was once a workmen's hut, but it has now been converted into a superior sheepfold. Below the enclosure is a pile of roofing slates, still as neatly stacked as on the day they were made, and nearby are several large lumps of rock drilled with holes ready for fence posts. The dressing floors, where the slate was split and shaped, are marked by slivers of waste rock, while more workings lie to the west.

Below you can see the widening in the beck that is Launchy Tarn, but to avoid the cliffs, head northwards along Bell Crags where easy grassy slopes lead through the rocky outcrops to Launchy Gill. It is not too boggy if you stay beside the stream and follow it down to the tarn, where the gill rushes over a little rocky shelf into the deeper water.

The map is deceptive, for though little more than a dub, Launchy Tarn is a most attractive place with the real atmosphere of a tarn, and as we ate our lunch beside it, two Red deer hinds watched us warily. The Thirlmere herd has migrated here from Martindale, and on every walk among these fells we have seen these elusive creatures. Most of the forest is fenced to exclude the deer, for they like to overwinter by browsing amongst the trees before venturing into the open to feed on grass for the rest of the year.

Thirlmere (*Divided lake*)

The meandering gill leads down to the edge of the trees, a delightful walk accompanied by the sound of the stream as it tumbles over the rocks. About sixty years ago this part of the forest was planted with Scots pine which is our only native forest conifer and likes rocky sites. Turning right beside the trees there is a short sharp climb, then it is an easy walk along the forest edge with

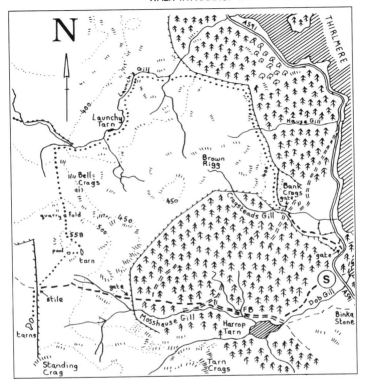

4.1

Helvellyn appearing so close that you can make out the tiny figures on the summit.

When Hause Gill is reached a narrow path is joined by some ruined barns and Thirlmere comes into view through the trees. Passing a perched boulder, follow the wall along above Bank Crags to where it goes steeply downhill. The angle is easier over to the right and you can zigzag down the grassy slope to a gate onto the forest road.

A little footpath keeps by the edge of the trees down to the metalled road, where the car park is only a few yards to the right, but it is more fitting first to walk down to the lake. Recently Thirlmere has been opened up to the public and 4 miles of lakeside paths have been constructed.

To return by the lake shore, cross the road to a kissing gate and follow an old lane down to the water's edge. A path then leads to the right through the trees beside the lake to the next little bay, where there is a footpath back to Dob Gill car park. This scenic road on the east shore of the lake was made by Manchester Corporation in 1889 after the level of the two small lakes of Leathes Water and Brackmere had been raised by 54ft to form Thirlmere Reservoir.

WALK 4.2: STEEL FELL AND GREENUP EDGE

Tarns:	Steel Fell Tarn (Rough Crag Tarn)
	Brownrigg Moss Tarn
	Greenup Edge Tarns
	Wythburn Head Tarns
Distance:	7 miles
Ascent:	1800ft
Summary:	Mountain walking with a very steep ascent, and a return down a deserted but boggy valley.
Starting Point:	(GR 321128) Wythburn. Car park by Thirlmere, on the minor road.

"Bottle sedge" said an expert from the Freshwater Biological Association, "is the characteristic plant that distinguishes a tarn from a lake." But what exactly is a bottle sedge and what does it look like? We didn't know, and we got out our book by the experts Richard and Alastair Fitter. Their volume on flowers was our mainstay; perhaps they could help us with the sedges.

At first sight a sedge looks pretty much like a grass, which makes things more difficult. Worldwide there are approximately 4000 species of sedge and around 10,000 different grasses. Even in this country there are so many of each that the task seemed impossible. There was bog sedge, spring sedge, glaucous sedge and oval sedge; there was brown sedge, white sedge and tawny sedge; there was even the starved wood sedge. Presumably this one would look rather pale and weedy, but fortunately it is rare in Britain so we could forget about it. Yet when tarn hunting how were we to find the bottle sedge among this host of look-alikes?

The first we found was cotton-grass, which despite its name is a sedge, but common cotton-grass and harestail cotton-grass, with their feathery plumes growing in the moorland bogs, were easily identified. Then there was pendulous sedge with its gracefully drooping catkin-like flowers - there's nothing else quite like it - but still the bottle sedge eluded us.

The day we had chosen for our exploration of Steel Fell, Greenup Edge

Thirlmere from Steel Fell

and Wythburn was dry, though brushing the fells the cloud played hide and seek with the tops. It was a steep climb to Steel Fell and then an easy plod along the ridge towards Calf Crag. Into the distance stretched the open moorland, with rushes, tussocks of grass and, no doubt, sedge.

Gradually gaining height towards Greenup Edge we entered the cloud. Now there was little to be seen and reaching the broad col, the very antithesis of an edge, a squelching bog entirely without landmarks, we turned northwards. A few pools glinted silver and beyond were the tarns. Unfrequented despite Wainwright's Coast to Coast Walk which passes over the col, they are off route and a pleasant place to relax.

It was at this point that we noticed the bottle sedge. At least we didn't know it was bottle sedge, but the plant that stood stiffly upright, nearly 3ft tall with its feet paddling in the water, was a striking sight. Like many of the sedges it had two flowers, the lower, female ones on short stalks, with above them the narrower dark brown male spikes, while the bracts, leaf-like extensions of the stem, stood highest of all.

We got out our book. We looked carefully through the pages. We looked through it again. There was no doubt about it, no other plant looked quite like this. The bottle sedge had been found.

The mist still hid from view all but our immediate surroundings as we retraced our steps to Flour Gill and made our way down to Wyth Burn and its tarn, but it had been a good day. We were well content.

ROUTE DESCRIPTION

Steel Fell (*Steep mountain*)

The steep grassy nose of Steel Fell almost reaches the lake shore and following the road from the end of the lake, over Stockhow Bridge, a bridleway leads off to Steel End Farm. When the village of Armboth and all the dwellings in the catchment area of the reservoir were demolished, only this farm, Wythburn church and the hamlet of Dalehead were spared.

Passing in front of the houses the path goes left beside the wall, then on entering the next field you turn up the hillside. It is a steep plod up the grassy spur beside the plantation, and Thirlmere soon appears beyond the trees. A gap in the top wall leads to the open fell and the route continues climbing up the grassy slopes of Steel Fell. The apparently dreary hillside is interesting to a botanist for amongst the more common wavy hair-grass and mat grass are the tufted spikes of deer grass, which confusingly is not a grass but a sedge. Heath woodrush, heath bedstraw and the small four-petalled yellow tormentil are all to be found here, along with the much rarer bog asphodel.

The angle relents as you near the fence, but the inviting rise ahead is not the top, for this lies nearly half a mile beyond. A step stile crosses the fence and from high above Ash Crags you can look down on Dunmail Raise where King Dunmail's burial cairn stands isolated in the middle of the dual

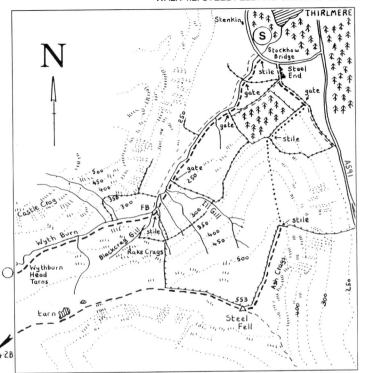

4.2A

carriageway. When the last King of Cumberland was killed in a battle with Malcolm, King of Scotland, and Edmund, King of the Saxons, in AD 945, the stones were piled upon him where he lay, and when the road was straightened and widened in 1971 the cairn was left untouched.

The fence is followed to the highest point of Steel Fell (1814ft) which is crowned by a small cairn beside an old fencepost. There is a fine view of Thirlmere which looks most attractive in spite of Ruskin's complaint that "Manchester is plotting to steal the waters of Thirlmere and the clouds of Helvellyn".

Steel Fell Tarn

The fence stretches on westwards to the first tarn of the day, which can be clearly seen from the summit of Steel Fell. Even in mist, navigation is little problem, as for much of the way you simply follow the fence. Passing a pool full of bogbean, the large peaty tarn is just beyond. This surprisingly extensive sheet of water sitting high on the ridge, though very shallow, contains cotton-grass, bogbean, three species of rush, and bottle sedge.

Brownrigg Moss Tarn (*Brown ridge bog tarn*)

Continuing along the broad ridge, with the occasional old metal fencepost for guidance, the path from the summit of Calf Crag is joined. A little way off to the right, the large shallow tarn sits in the middle of the flat grassy ridge of Brownrigg Moss, surrounded by glacial moraines.

Greenup Edge Tarns (*Tarns on the edge of the green valley*)

Passing to the left of a little knoll, the path now follows the rim of the Far Easedale valley, and dips to the lowest point, where you turn right to follow the boggy path westwards across the head of the Wythburn valley. The path is rather vague in places and it looks a long way to the skyline, but it is an easy enough climb. A steady stream of Coast to Coast walkers, heading for Robin Hood's Bay, indicate the route, which is now much more obvious than it was in the days of H.H. Symonds when he wrote "Queer divagations have occurred on Greenup".

At the col of Greenup Edge turn right along the ridge path towards Ullscarf, then after passing a row of three little pools the pair of tarns is reached. Much silted up with bottle sedge they were obviously once a good deal larger and may originally have been one. The adjacent rocky outcrop with a cairn gives a good view of the Wythburn valley and of the high fells, with Skiddaw to the north, Helvellyn to the east, and in the west the lumpy shape of Great Gable.

Wythburn Head Tarns (*Tarns at the top of willow tree valley*)

The direct descent to Wyth Burn is very steep, so it is safer to retrace your steps to the col and follow Flour Gill down. The valley, where sphagnum moss flourishes, is the site of a former tarn and it is well named "The Bog", but the banks of the gill give a comparatively dry passage unless it has been very wet when it is advisable to keep to the surrounding higher ground. Reaching a ruined sheepfold beside the gill, a little path follows the stream down past a second sheepfold.

The grandly named Wythburn Head Tarns lie in an area of hummocky mounds where the beck splashes into a deep placid pool, and although it is little more than a widening of the river, the yellow water-lilies, known locally as brandy bottles from the shape of their seed heads, make a most attractive setting.

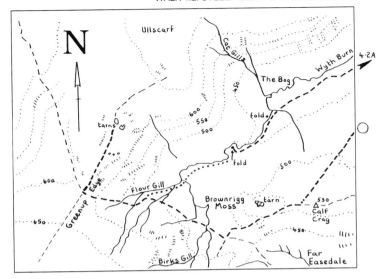

4.2B

Wythburn Valley

The Wyth Burn then hurries on down, the path broadens under Black Crag, and this part of the valley is delightful with rocky cliffs and little waterfalls. Passing a bridge the path goes through walled enclosures, where in July there are masses of the golden starlike flowers of bog asphodel, which was once used by the ladies of Lancashire to dye their hair yellow.

Staying by the burn the concession path then follows it back through the fields below Steel End to reach Stockhow Bridge and the road. Thirlmere may be very different from its former days, but as the MP Isaac Fletcher pointed out a century ago, the construction of the reservoir preserved the valley and stopped wealthy businessmen from building their "Gothic villas upon the shores of this beautiful lake".

5: Grasmere Tarns

WALK 5.1: SERGEANT MAN AND EASEDALE TARN

Tarns:	Ash Crags Tarn
	Codale Head Tarns
	Sergeant Man Tarn
	Codale Tarn
	Easedale Tarn
Distance:	7½ miles
Ascent:	2200ft
Summary:	A good mountain walk to a favourite tarn, but the navigation can be tricky in mist.
Starting Point:	(GR 335080) Easedale Road, Grasmere. The small car park soon fills up, extra parking in the village, 10 minutes' walk away.

"I really must go there some day" said the farmer's wife with whom we were staying. She had been born, brought up and lived all her life within a stone's throw of Easedale Tarn, but as yet, she confessed, hadn't got round to a visit.

Easedale Tarn must be one of the most visited tarns in all Lakeland, for it is little more than a mile from the road, and struggling up the path beside Sourmilk Gill there is usually a constant flow of walkers, some dressed for the mountains, but more often in clothes that look surprised by the Lakeland rain. The young men we met one evening, carrying great armfuls of gear up the path from Grasmere, didn't think it too distant. They had planned to be comfortable and they wouldn't lack entertainment, for among their possessions was a very large 'ghetto-blaster'.

As the evening grew darker we could see them busily at work fetching dead branches, and dragging them back to the sheepfold they had selected as a home. Then as twilight slowly darkened into night, shadowy shapes moved in silhouette, outlined by the flames of their campfire, while faintly over the water came the sounds of their music.

Codale Tarn is more for connoisseurs. A little off the main path climbing to Sergeant Man, it is less often the objective of a walk and the circular hollow surrounded by mountains is occupied by small brown trout, brought here countless years ago to provide sport for fishermen. It is now too far for most anglers and the only disadvantage is that the sun sets early, sinking behind the slopes of Sergeant Man and High Raise. But it is a delightful spot. A solitary tree stands beside its dark blue waters, there are a few sheep, and

Sourmilk Gill

hopefully no ghetto-blasters.

John Bolton was not put off by a little discomfort. An enthusiastic amateur seeker of fossils in the mid-nineteenth century, he was in the habit of going on expeditions alone. In the following account describing a night spent on the fells, he refers constantly to himself as 'we'. This is mere poetic licence for he had no companion and the entire expedition was a solitary affair:

The first thing to look out for was a lodging, but there being no friendly nooks among the rocks, we went forward to an old sheep-fold we had seen in a former ramble. This was a square inclosure, the walls being about five feet high, and the ground wet and miry all over. There was a sort of gateway on the east side, and an old gate was lying on the ground. We carried this to the west or sheltered side of the inclosure, to be used as a bedstead, and not a bad one either, only it was about three feet too short, but we were thankful for it as it would keep us out of the wet and mire which covered the whole place.

We now began to prepare supper, which was also our dinner, for we had eaten nothing all day; but as the sheep-fold was high up the hillside, there was nothing but bog water within a considerable distance, so we filled the half-pint can with this, put the coffee and sugar into it cold, then lit a fire and sat down on the little gate (in the same way that a tailor sits at his work) and ate our supper with a thankful heart.

The next day it started to rain, and despite digging a trench with his geological hammer and huddling under an umbrella, he was soon thoroughly soaked. It was a wild retreat to the valley, during which he had to lie flat on the ground to avoid being blown over. A tough enough expedition for anyone, but John Bolton was then in his 74th year.

ROUTE DESCRIPTION

Easedale (*Esa's valley*)

Easedale Road leads out of Grasmere village and a permissive path avoids the road walking as far as Goody Bridge. The road continues through an open field, and the tarmac comes to an end at a cluster of houses. Taking the rough track ('Not for cars') go through an iron gate, and keeping left, the stone flanked track follows the edge of the fields. Ahead is the silver ribbon of Sourmilk Gill, which Dorothy Wordsworth called 'Churn Milk Force', and the valley was a favourite haunt of William and Dorothy who named Easedale 'The Black Quarter' because of its evening shadows when seen from their home at Dove Cottage.

Far Easedale

The stone walled track passes a couple of barns and then continues up the valley beside Far Easedale Gill. The old stepping stones at Stythwaite Steps have been supplemented by a footbridge, and the path climbs on up Far

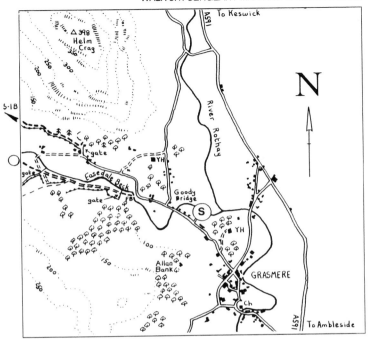

5.1A

Easedale beneath the steep, bracken covered slopes of Helm Crag. Though the route follows Wainwright's popular Coast to Coast Walk from Rosthwaite to Grasmere, you are unlikely to meet many people early in the day.

It is a long but easy walk up Far Easedale, with the craggy slopes of Gibson Knott and Calf Crag to the right, and the cliffs of Deer Bields rising to the left. Deer Bields Buttress, for many years one of the 'last great problems' in rock climbing, was finally led by Arthur Dolphin on 24th June 1951 and graded Extreme.

The path then steepens to pass a series of pretty waterfalls and, crossing the gill, continues to climb. Beside the path is a small plaque to Kevin Charles Smith 1960-1991, but the site of the memorial is a mystery, for Stewart Hulse, the leader of the Langdale Mountain Rescue Team, says that there is no record of any fatality here. Climbing on past Ferngill Crag and Broadstone Head, the col is reached, where a lonely stile over a non-existent fence leads on to Borrowdale.

105

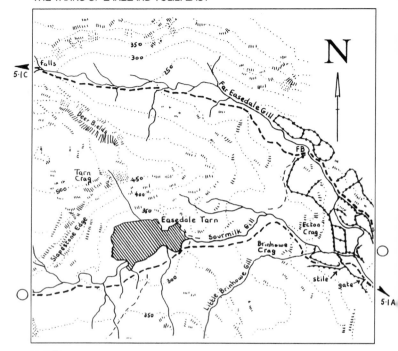

5.1B

Ash Crags Tarn

Turning now left, follow the fence uphill on an indistinct path through the peat hags. As the path climbs beside Mere Beck it soon becomes more obvious, bending away from the stream before returning again to squeeze through a rocky pass. The stream below flows in the narrow ravine of Deep Slack and as this comes to an end, you turn left to climb pathless grass to the little tarn on the ridge. So close, yet hidden from sight, this tarn is one of those delightful surprises that the Lake District has in store, with views of blue water, rocky knolls, and the distant mountains of Helvellyn and Fairfield.

Codale Head Tarns

Returning to the path and past a higher pool, continue to climb by the occasional fencepost, and then passing another small pool, the first of the

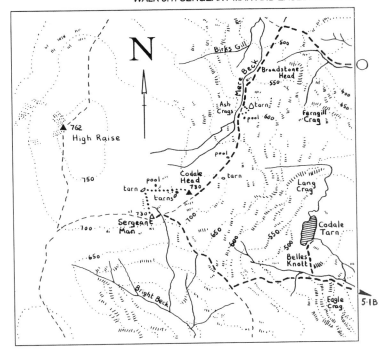

5.1C

Codale Head Tarns lies on a grassy shelf a couple of hundred yards beyond. Codale Head itself, a rocky knoll with a cairn, and a separate 2000ft top for peak baggers, is bypassed by the path, but fenceposts lead to the summit (2395ft), and beyond, in a rather marshy hollow, are another couple of tarns.

Sergeant Man Tarn (*Tarn by Sergeant's cairn*)

Passing to the right of the twin tarns, head west by a tempting pool, really too small to be a tarn, then rounding a rocky knoll the next tarn appears. The tarn, which is quite large with a stony bed and surrounded by gentle grassy slopes, is also on the line of the ruined fence, which continues westwards towards High Raise.

Sergeant Man

The ancient boundary is now abandoned to head south to the distinctive

107

summit of Sergeant Man (2395ft). This rocky knoll occupies a commanding position and though really only the end of a ridge running down from High Raise and not a separate mountain at all, it is the objective of many walks from the valley. With few obvious landmarks to follow in the mist, we have met more 'lost' walkers on these fells than anywhere else in Lakeland.

In clear weather Sergeant Man is, however, a good viewpoint and the tarns provide pointers to the distant summits. The summit of Helvellyn appears beyond the twin tarns of Codale Head, while above Sergeant Man Tarn lies Skiddaw. To the south are the rocky crags of Pavey Ark and Harrison Stickle, and the skyline continues westwards over Crinkle Crags, Bow Fell and the Scafells to the pudding shape of Great Gable. But for the walk to Stickle Tarn, which lies far below, you will have to buy Volume1!

Codale Tarn

The main path goes eastwards across a small stream and then descends south-east. Reaching a large flat slab, Easedale Tarn comes into view and the path continues downhill. As the ridge levels out, watch for a sharp turn left, where a well-cairned path descends steeply into the valley.

Codale Tarn is off the main path, and disappears from sight as you get closer, but aiming for the shelf on which it lies, turn left to join the little path that goes to the tarn. Set beneath the rocky outcrops of Lang Crag, this quiet tarn, which has a rock for an island, is fed by a stream and the outflow tumbles into a miniature gorge before falling steeply past Belles Knott into the valley below.

Easedale Tarn

Returning along the small path around Belles Knott which, though of no consequence from above, presents an interesting rocky pyramid to the east, the main path is rejoined. The descent is quite steep at first, but after the two streams have merged it is then a gentle stroll past the rocky amphitheatre formed by Eagle Crag and Blea Crag.

Easedale Tarn is one of the loveliest mountain tarns in the Lakes and a favourite walk from Grasmere. Described by de Quincy as "the most gloomily sublime", it actually feels very open, with bracken covered slopes sweeping down to grassy mounds of glacial moraine, and roche moutoner, whose rounded glacier smoothed shapes indeed resemble a recumbent Herdwick. Above the tarn stands the rocky prow of Tarn Crag, and on the far shore there is a sheepfold, while beside a large boulder above the outflow are the remains of the refreshment hut mentioned in many old guidebooks, demolished some thirty years ago by volunteers.

Grasmere (*Grassy lake*)

The path, which has been attractively pitched by the National Trust, descends to the right of Sourmilk Gill with a fine view of Helm Crag across the Easedale valley. The waterfall is a series of delightful cascades and growing by the stream are clumps of juniper. The berries are used as a flavouring in cooking, though strictly they are not berries at all but fleshy and juicy versions of tiny pine cones.

It would be difficult now to get lost, as the path leads down into Easedale and through a kissing gate into fields, which in spring are full of lambs. Continuing beside Easedale Beck, and then across a stream, go through the leftmost of two gates and beside the beck until two footbridges lead to Easedale Road, where you turn right back to Grasmere village, the tourists and the tea shops.

WALK 5.2: ALCOCK TARN

Tarns:	Alcock Tarn
	Whitemoss Tarn
	How Top Tarn
Distance:	3 miles
Ascent:	1000ft
Summary	A Wordsworth walk. A steep climb with beautiful views of Grasmere.
Starting Point:	(GR 340073) Grasmere. Stock Lane car park.

Often in her *Journal* Dorothy Wordsworth refers to walking, sometimes alone, more usually with her brother, and when one November she notes regretfully "We did not walk. William said he would put it off till the fine moonlight night, and then it came on heavy rain and wind", it is as though somehow the day was incomplete.

Yet on their many walks there is never a mention of Alcock Tarn. Set high on a shelf on the steep hillside of Heron Pike, it is only a mile from Dove Cottage. But a hundred years were to pass before Mr Alcock dammed the moss beneath Butter Crag, and the long and narrow tarn was yet to appear when William, in his poem *Michael*, wrote of the ascent "Up the tumultuous brook of Green-head Ghyll".

The poem about an old shepherd, his son Luke and the bond they made at the sheepfold beside Greenhead Gill was one that gave William a great deal of difficulty. Dorothy often wrote of him "working at the sheepfold", though this refers to the poem rather than to the circle of tumbled stones that inspired his verse. After a month's effort William destroyed what he had written, but starting again he had more success, and the lines we know today were completed on 9th December 1800.

Anne at Alcock Tarn

By 17th December Dorothy notes "writing all day for William", for she would copy out the finished poems, but sometimes they were not quite complete. Mrs Nicholson, the old Ambleside postmistress loved to tell how brother and sister would appear at her house late at night, in order to make some alteration to a manuscript that had already been posted: *At that time said Mrs N, the mail used to pass through at one in the morning so my husband and I used to go early to bed; but when Mr and Miss W. came, let it be as late as it would, my husband would get up and let them in and give them their letter out of the box, and then they would sit up in our parlour or in the kitchen discussing over it and reading and changing till they had made it quite to their minds, and then they would say 'Now Mr. Nicholson, please would you bolt the door after us? Here is our letter for the post. We'll not trouble you any more this night'.*

Reading Dorothy's journal, written between May 1800 and January 1803, with its delightful picture of day to day life in Grasmere, and her sharp,

WALK 5.2: ALCOCK TARN

fresh observation of nature, the creativity of William's seems at times to merge with hers. Dorothy records with delight on a March morning in 1803:

While we were at breakfast - he, with his basin of broth before him untouched, and a little plate of bread and butter he wrote the Poem to a Butterfly! He ate not a morsel, nor put on his stockings, but sate with his shirt neck unbuttoned, and his waistcoat open while he did it. The thought first came upon him as we were talking about the pleasure we both always feel at the sight of a butterfly. I told him that I used to chase them a little, but that I was afraid of brushing the dust off their wings.

And Dorothy's words find echo in her brother's poem

*But she, God love her! feared to brush
The dust from off its wings*

The way in which Dorothy sees, sometimes her very words, are transcribed by William into poetry. But is the creativity his or hers? She had the vision, he turned it into verse, and when her flame died then his died too. For though she lived until the age of 80, her last years were in a fog which modern experts have called Alzheimer's disease, while William, by now a famous poet, had lost the muse and, though made Poet Laureate, never again composed the poems that had been their common bond. "She gave me eyes. She gave me ears." It was a gift that Wordsworth never forgot.

ROUTE DESCRIPTION

Greenhead Gill (*Stream with the green upper end*)

Heading into Grasmere village, turn aside into the churchyard to see the simple graves of the Wordsworth family. Leaving by the lych-gate, past the famous gingerbread shop, once the old schoolhouse where Wordsworth himself taught, keep straight on to the little green and Sam Read's Bookshop and turn right along Broadgate.

After crossing the River Rothay, fork right up Swan Lane to the main road. Passing to the right of the Swan Hotel, the inn visited surreptitiously by Sir Walter Scott when staying with the abstemious Wordsworths, follow the road round to the left, then turn up the footpath 'to Alcock Tarn and Greenhead Gill'.

A narrow tarmac track leads beside the "tumultuous brook", and after the private bridge, you go through a gate and over a little footbridge. The climb now begins in earnest, and one can sympathise with Heaton Cooper's guests who were brought this way for a trial of their "mountain form".

A newly stepped way leads up past a wooden seat and above a little reservoir which is on the line of the aqueduct from Thirlmere to Manchester. To the left bracken covered slopes drop steeply to the gill and looking back there is a grand view of Helm Crag, with the rocks, known affectionately as the Lion and the Lamb, outlined on the summit. Below in the valley is a trial level, but the Grasmere Lead Mine, which was worked for about ten years from 1564, lies out of sight round the corner.

The path continues climbing steeply, with Grasmere village laid out below. You can see the full length of Greenhead Gill and the piled stones which may be Michael's sheepfold, "Beside the brook appears a straggling heap of unhewn stones!", or they may, more prosaically, be the remains of the Elizabethan lead mine.

Alcock Tarn

Gradually the angle eases, and above are the shattered outcrops of Butter Crag. The Guides Race at Grasmere Sports, held on the third Thursday in August, is to the top of these cliffs, ¾ mile each way. Time to the top 10 minutes. Time down again less than 3!

A wall is reached with a stile over a wired gate and ahead is Alcock Tarn. Originally called Buttercrags Tarn, the name was changed at the beginning of the century when Mr Alcock of The Hollins, a large house in the valley below, enlarged a small reservoir and stocked it with trout. Grassy banks within the enclosing wall slope down to this clear little tarn, described by Wainwright as 'a dreary sheet of water'. But he must have come on a bad day, for from the dam, which is now in need of repair, there is a splendid view out across Grasmere to the low hills at the foot of Langdale, while beyond are the higher fells, the Langdale Pikes, Bow Fell and Wetherlam.

The neighbouring Dockey Tarn, which lies to the south-east on a shelf below a little pointed cliff, can be reached by contouring along the hillside, but it is disappointing and not worth the effort as we have yet to find any water covering its few blackened stones.

Whitemoss Tarn

From the dam a path turns right, through a gap in the wall, to the rocky knoll of Grey Crag, a splendid summit of which many a mountain would be proud. To the left is a very grand sheepfold, which has recently been repaired, and beside it is a trough for dipping sheep. The path bends back to cross the beck and you descend the fell, with Grasmere beneath your feet, on the old pony road which was built by Mr Harwood, a later resident of The Hollins, for his invalid wife.

After passing a small ornamental pool the path curves left above the trees, by a memorial seat, to enter the wood at a gate. The track goes through the trees to another gate, where you turn right along an old road for a few yards. A footpath then leads beside the wall to join the road by the drive of Heugh Folds, where a few yards to the left along the tarmac is Whitemoss Tarn. Shadowed by rhododendrons, and still much overgrown despite the efforts of John Wyatt who tried to clear it some years ago when he was Chief Ranger of the National Park, the narrow tarn had just enough open water for a pair of mallards. Dorothy Wordsworth describes White Moss as a place of

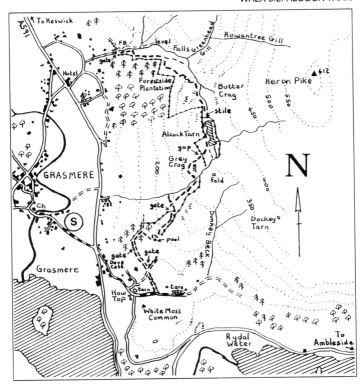

5.2

"fairy valleys and fairy tarns" and it may have been here that she encountered the "leech-gatherer".

How Top Tarn (*Hill top tarn*)

Follow the lane back and down to the junction, then turn right at How Top past a little tarn. Most writers describe this as a duck pond which seems very unfair as it is quite large, very attractive and full of water, which is more than you can say about Dockey Tarn. If you are lucky there may even be some ducks. Dorothy Wordsworth tells of a funeral at How Top Farm in 1800: "They talked sensibly and chearfully about common things".

The road, which was the original turnpike from Rydal to Grasmere, descends to the hamlet of Town End, past Dove Cottage. This was the first home of William and Dorothy to which they came in 1799, and as Norman Nicholson says, "You can imagine a female relative in every room industriously copying out poems". When John Major visited Dove Cottage in 1993, the staff were taken by surprise and the director had to quickly put on a suit. Crossing this modern main road you walk back down Stock Lane into Grasmere, but don't, like Mr Major, leave without buying your Grasmere gingerbread.

Nymphaea alba

6: Ambleside Tarns

WALK 6.1: LOUGHRIGG FELL

Tarns:	Loughrigg Tarn
	Loughrigg Fell Tarns
	Lily Tarn
Distance:	4 miles
Ascent:	1000ft
Summary:	A beautiful fellwalk best saved for a fine day.
Starting Point:	(GR 345039) The road junction to the south of Loughrigg Tarn at Tarn Foot. Roadside parking.

We had come on the wrong day. Loughrigg Fell lay under a softly enveloping blanket of grey, it was cold and damp, the mist was down to the road, and there was nothing to be seen. The fell, however, seemed to be remarkably popular. There was barely room to squeeze our car onto the verge, and no sooner had we done so than two Landrovers arrived bringing yet more people. Standing about in groups, figures surveyed the scene, then pulling on waterproofs and boots, set off purposefully up the fellside.

In the distance came the faint sound of dogs. It was March, a month belonging to the foxhunting season, which lasts from October to May, and these were the Coniston Foxhounds. Now housed at Rydal, they cover Langdale, Coniston and the Furness Fells, and as with all Lakeland packs the hunters follow on foot, and only the huntsman wears a scarlet coat.

Undoubtedly the appeal of foxhunting is in the chase, for whether it is a hound-trail, or the pursuit of a fox, the dogs at full stretch streaking across the fellside are a magnificent sight. That the fox, a beautiful red-brown elegant animal, is to be caught and killed is to many abhorrent, yet to most farmers it is the reason for the hunt, and when you have seen the pathetic bodies of little lambs lying on the fellside, and heard the farmer's bitter comment that the fox had another three last night, you can see both sides.

"Well" we said, "as we're here we may as well make the most of it", and set off steeply uphill into the gloom. It was quiet, almost eerily quiet, with just the faintest of breezes stirring the mist. Then without warning the dogs were upon us. Dark grey shapes hurtled out of nowhere, were past in an instant, and vanished into nothing. There was no sound save the whisper of pads on the turf, the gasp of lungs straining for air, and the skittering sound of small stones dislodged by the eager pursuit. In the distance a yelp was followed by another and then answered by a horn.

The Langdale Pikes from Loughrigg Tarn

At one time individual farmers set traps and snares, but then they banded together to keep packs of specially bred hounds. As well as the Coniston Foxhounds there are still another five packs in the Lakes. The rough Wast Water mountains are the hunting ground of the Eskdale and Ennerdale hounds, while the famous Melbreak pack hunts among the North-Western Fells. Around Keswick it is the Blencathra hounds; the fells of Patterdale and Mardale are covered by the Ullswater hounds, and the Lunesdale hounds hunt the eastern moors outside the National Park.

Though little over 1000ft in height, and barely a square mile in extent, there is more scenery packed into Loughrigg Fell than practically anywhere else in Lakeland. One glance at the map shows it all. The contours are hidden beneath a tangle of black lines denoting rocks, while meandering across the fellside, streams dissect the area into a multitude of separate kingdoms. The rocks are not large, but in mist the fell is full of surprises, with every hummock and hollow conspiring to confuse.

Tarn hunting in the mist on Loughrigg Fell is a challenge and it is even more of a challenge when there is a foxhunt going on at the same time. Tarns appeared and vanished as silently as the hounds and only careful compass work and pacing led us to the small glassy pools fringed with reeds. But there was something strange about Lily Tarn. Standing at the water's edge was a creation, a sculpture, a mass of old and knotted boughs woven together into a primeval shape. Seated beside it was a group of students in earnest conversation. They looked more like strange and wandering figures from a past century, but their voices gave them away. "Cambridge, actually" they said.

ROUTE DESCRIPTION
Loughrigg Tarn (*Tarn on the ridge above the lake*)
A metalled lane leads up from the road junction to the farm at Tarn Foot and the bridleway, signed 'To the Tarn', passes in front of the cottages. In a few yards go through the gate on the left and along the Drive, once a private carriage road built by Mr Wheatley-Balme, an off-comer and wealthy businessman from Mirefield in Yorkshire, who bought High Close in 1857. His money helped rebuild the church and school at Chapel Stile, and when he died he left his house, now a Youth Hostel, to the National Trust.

The still waters of Loughrigg Tarn, described by Wordsworth as "Diana's Looking-glass", are frequented by swans, while in the distance is the familiar outline of the Langdale Pikes. The tarn, which is encircled by a concession path, can be reached by going over a little stile and the track rejoined by the cottages at the How.

Loughrigg Fell (*Ridge above the lake*)
About 100 yards after the cottages, a gate leads onto Loughrigg Fell, and a

footpath contours round the hillside keeping above the wall. Reaching the trees, turn up the fell and it is a steep climb by a little stream until the main path is joined close to the summit of Loughrigg Fell. This was our son Jeremy's first unaided summit, reached at the age of nearly four. Though at only a little over 1000ft perched by the stone OS trig column high above Grasmere, you feel on top of the world, with a view which inspired four whole pages from Wainwright. As he said, "anybody spending a first holiday in Ambleside cannot do better than make an early visit to the top of Loughrigg Fell".

Loughrigg Fell Tarns

In the Ice Age the undulating top of the fell was scraped clean by glaciers, leaving a landscape of bare rocky outcrops and boggy hollows, now occupied by an assortment of tarns and pools. Retrace your steps to the junction below the summit then, heading south-east, continue downhill along the main path which descends steeply to a little spring. Here, within yards of the path, the lovely yellow mountain saxifrage can be found. Though not rare by botanical standards, *Saxifraga azoides* is a lot less common in the Lakes than in Scotland where it forms spreading golden carpets in the bogs. The first of the little tarns, shallow and surrounded by reeds, moss and bog, is then about 150 yards off to the left.

Returning through the knolls to the main path, follow it south-east, then approaching a wall the path climbs briefly and swings east to the second, and larger, member of the Loughrigg Fell tarns. Accompanied by a retinue of small pools, the shallow stretch of water is surrounded by rocky knolls and dotted with tiny grassy islands.

The path climbs briefly and heading south-east again, descends with Windermere ahead. Joining a more obvious path, continue down to cross a stream in a valley beside a small peaty pool. A grassy path now climbs the hill opposite, still heading south-east, and nearly at the top, set between rocky knolls, is another little tarn with a good display of bog asphodel and cotton-grass.

Lily Tarn

Continuing east down to a kissing gate, the path heads on over the fell top, and keeping to the left of the wall past Todd Crag, Lily Tarn appears ahead. This is the biggest of the fell-top tarns, and as well as bogbean, whose lovely pink and white flowers make even the most prosaic puddle a delight in spring, there is a small island and the white water-lilies after which the tarn is named. The grassy banks are a pleasant place to linger and though it is less than a mile to the thronging streets of Ambleside you will probably have it all to yourself.

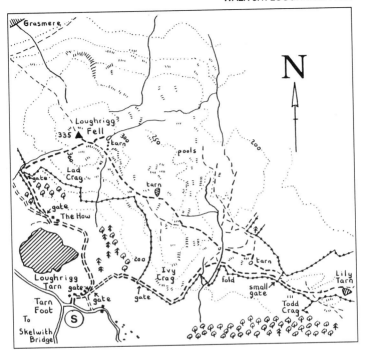

6.1

Tarn Foot

Retrace your steps to the kissing gate, then follow the path above the wall and fork left over a stream to join the main path. This leads down beside the wall beneath Ivy Crag which Jonathon Otley's 1832 *Guide to the Lakes* urged you to climb for "an instantaneous burst upon a most extraordinary assemblage of landscape beauties". The path becomes a track signed Elterwater and Langdale which takes you back to Tarn Foot, and if there is time, a visit to Skelwith Force and the Kirkstone Galleries makes an excellent end to the day.

WALK 6.2: SCANDALE TARN AND RED SCREES

Tarns:	Scandale Tarn
	Red Screes Tarn
Distance:	8 miles
Ascent:	2550ft
Summary:	A quiet fell walk to a little visited tarn and a mountain summit.
Starting Point:	(GR 377046) Ambleside, by the Salutation Inn. Long stay car park on the Grasmere road.

Leaving Ambleside behind we began the gentle climb to Scandale Tarn. Up the road past the Charlotte Mason College, where our niece trained as a teacher; up through the woods where the path is like a tunnel through the trees; on past Low Sweden Bridge, which has nothing to do with Scandinavia, but is a corruption of St Swithen; and up into the long valley of Scandale Beck. Surprisingly the name means the short valley, but it seems long, and on either hand stone walls rise straight, unerringly up the fellsides towards the ridges high above.

> *The wall walks the fell-*
> *Grey millipede on slow*
> *Stone hooves;*
> *Its slack back hollowed*
> *At gulleys and grooves,*

Norman Nicholson captures the spirit, but these walls are remarkably straight. Unlike the wriggling boundaries that separate the tiny valley fields, with never a straight line where three curving ones will do, the fellside walls above the Scandale Beck deviate not an inch from the mathematically direct line. They date, of course, from the Enclosure Acts.

Before the beginning of the nineteenth century, land was often owned in common. All the local families had the right to pasture their cattle and sheep, each eking out a simple, self-sufficient existence. But there was no incentive to improve and gradually the soil became increasingly poor and unproductive. What was needed, said some of the go-ahead landowners, was enclosure.

Walls, of course, were nothing new to the Lakeland fells. The heavy, thick Wasdale boundaries date back to the tenth century, while in Eskdale they can be traced precisely to 1284, when the monks enclosed their sheep pastures. Even on the Fairfield Horseshoe the wall that follows the crest of the ridge was built in the year 1277, when the valley of Rydal Beck was enclosed to form a deer park. But until the beginning of the nineteenth century most of the high fells were still free open land.

Enclosure started gradually. Piecemeal applications from landowners

Caiston Beck

were considered in isolation until, in 1801, an Act of Parliament was passed. The process was heavily weighted in favour of the larger landowners, for any objection had to be presented to Parliament either by a solicitor or in person. The poor man who pastured a few sheep or cattle on the common ground was thus unable to make himself heard, and when the enclosures took place, and the land was allocated, the rules which demanded each should pay his share of the costs effectively eliminated anyone without capital. Thus in a short period of time land passed from a common holding to the ownership of a small number of wealthy landowners, and the dispossessed had little choice but to work as labourers for their new masters.

It seems harsh, and indeed it was, but with enclosure came progress. Now with the possibility of segregating animals, tups from ewes, and one flock from another, controlled breeding developed, and new methods of agriculture. For centuries as winter approached, all but next year's stock of breeding animals would be killed and their meat salted down. But now land could be used to cultivate fodder for the winter months, rotational cropping was introduced and manuring of the land improved the soil. It was the Agricultural Revolution and it was to change the face of the Lake District.

The walls were the key, and the enclosure acts were very precise in specifying how they were to be built:

34 inches broad in the bottom and 6 feet high, under a stone not exceeding 4 inches in thickness - there shall be laid in a workman-like manner 21 good throughs in every rood of fence, and the first 12 to be laid on at a height of 2 feet broad, and the second 9 to be laid on at the height of 4 feet from the ground.

Little wonder then that nearly 200 years later the "stone fences" still stand, mile after mile, traversing the fellside. But we have grown used to them, and if perhaps in places they are beginning to look a little tired and worn, maybe it is a sign that this is the end of an era and soon the mountains will once again be free to all.

ROUTE DESCRIPTION

High Sweden Bridge (*St Swithen's bridge or the land cleared by burning*)
Starting at the Salutation Inn in the centre of Ambleside, walk up North Road, once an old packhorse route, and turn right up Kirkstone Road. The first turning on the left is Sweden Bridge Lane and this leads gently uphill past the houses. The tarmac comes to an end at a gate, and the rough track climbs on up the hillside. Views westwards are of Rydal Water and the slopes of Low Pike, the final summit of the Fairfield Horseshoe. This is the most direct route from Ambleside to Patterdale and in 1933 was described by Symonds as "admirably quiet and pastoral, with a touch in it of higher things".

The trees are entered at a gate where the steep wooded slopes of Low Sweden Coppice drop to Scandale Beck and in the spring primroses bloom

6.2A

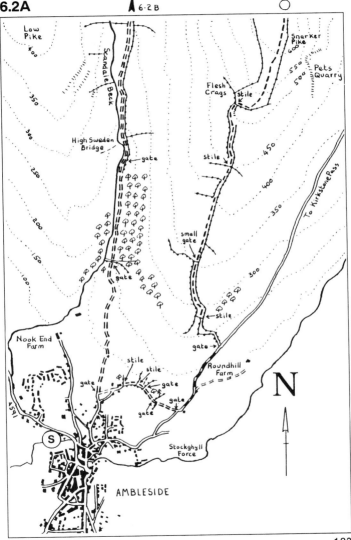

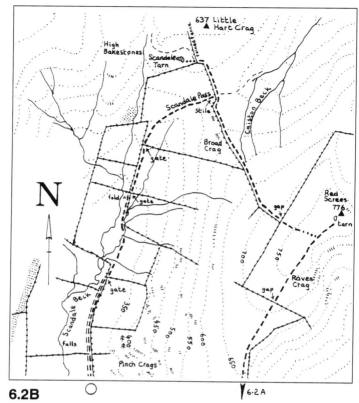

6.2B

in places inaccessible to the sheep. High Sweden Bridge is everything a packhorse bridge should be. Built two, or even three, centuries ago, it has not been spoilt by the addition of a parapet which was often added as a safety measure when the era of the pack ponies, with their wide panniers, came to an end.

Scandale Tarn (*Short valley tarn*)

As we squeezed past a JCB laying concrete drains, we were reminded that this broad track is maintained by the National Park, and it makes for easy gentle walking beside the beck. The valley was smoothed to its wide U-shape in the Ice Age, and below a little waterfall are hummocks of glacial moraines which were dumped by the retreating ice. The end of the flat valley is reached at Scandale Bottom where a stream is forded, then passing a sheepfold the path climbs the rib between two streams beside a wall.

After a final gate the climb begins in earnest up the Scandale Pass. This ancient way was not used much after the alternative route was made over the Kirkstone Pass, for it climbs an extra 300ft. Crossing the ladder stile at the col, turn left and continue to climb beside the wall, which as it reaches Scandale Tarn bends away downhill. There is a long view down the valley of Scandale Beck to Windermere, to the north-east lie the twin rocky tops of Little Hart Crag, while on the skyline above the tarn is one of the surviving stone men of High Bakestones, where five of the eight cairns were destroyed in 1994. While many pass within yards of the tarn, few turn aside even for a moment to the quiet grassy bowl where a little stream hurries down to join Scandale Beck.

Red Screes Tarn

Retracing your steps to the col, keep straight on and follow the wall up the steep slopes of Red Screes. It is a stiff ascent of 900ft, and as you climb past the flat slabs of Broad Crag, Brothers Water with its square field of tents comes into view. When the wall turns away towards Middle Dodd, continue climbing in the same direction to join the ridge, where you turn left past a pool to the little mountain tarn.

Red Screes Tarn on the grassy summit, and only 20 yards from the stone OS trig point (2549ft), must be the nearest tarn to a mountain top in the Lakes. Yet it never seems to dry up in spite of the fact that it is replenished almost entirely by rain water. There are splendid views down the Kirkstone Pass, which De Quincy claimed in 1785 to have descended in about 6 minutes, a speed he calculated to be at least 18 miles per hour. The pass acquired its name from a rock near the road which resembles a church, and the steepest part of the pass was called 'The Struggle' where passengers in the horse-drawn carriages to Patterdale had to get out and walk.

Ambleside

The descent now lies to the south and walking back along the ridge there is a bird's-eye view of the Kirkstone Inn, while rising above it, like rows of stage scenery, two ridges converge on Caudale Moor, beyond is the switchback of Froswick and Ill Bell while furthest, and on the skyline, is the Cross Fell Range.

It is a gentle way down, heading towards the end of Windermere, following the path past the top of Raven Crag and by a large cairn, then keeping beside a wall to Snarker Pike, Ambleside appears below, and on the far horizon is the sea.

The path continues down the broad ridge above Pet's Quarry, which re-

High Sweden Bridge

opened in 1950 and is one of the few quarries still working in the Lakes, then meeting a wall you turn right to a ladder stile and down between the walls of a wide green lane. This was an 'occupation' road along which cattle and sheep were herded up onto the fells. With a final steep descent the footpath reaches the Kirkstone Road, and this is followed for about ¼ mile before turning right at the bend opposite a hotel, on the footpath to Ellerigg.

The gated walled track leads by a memorial seat, with a good view over Ambleside, and passing a Christmas tree plantation, goes along the edge of the fields to a little gate onto Ellerigg Road. Sweden Bridge Lane then takes you down into the town, but you can vary the route back by exploring Old Ambleside where Rattle Gill recalls the noise once made by the mills and waterwheels of Stock Ghyll.

WALK 6.3: MIDDLERIGG TARN

Tarns:	Middlerigg Tarn
Distance:	3¹/₂ miles
Ascent:	650ft
Summary:	Quiet tracks link Brockhole and Town End. In the season Brockhole is open every day and Town End each afternoon, except Saturday and Monday.
Starting Point:	(GR 391010) Brockhole, on the A591 between Ambleside and Windermere. Car park.
Alternative Start:	(GR 405019) Minor road near Town End, parking in layby.

After a week in a Lakeland cottage somehow there always seems to be more to take home than we brought, and the car bulged with our possessions. We didn't want to waste the last day, but with crime on the increase, the chance of our luggage vanishing from a town car park or roadside layby seemed a distinct possibility.

The solution was a walk from Brockhole, for surely the car would be safe there. So leaving our vehicle near the ticket machine in an empty car park the size of a playing field, we set off with hardly a backward glance. Middlerigg Tarn, though private, is well seen from the bridleway that links Troutbeck to Brockhole, and with the weather less than perfect, this was a chance to combine tarn bagging with a visit to two stately homes.

Town End, a typical Lakeland yeoman's house, is one of our favourite National Trust properties. We arrived just as the house was opening its doors and the gloomy afternoon was brightened by a welcoming log fire. The ladies in the kitchen looked so comfortably installed that, for a brief moment, we were deluded into thinking they lived here, but no, they were guides waiting to show the visitors round. The house, which was built around 1626, has remained virtually unchanged over the centuries, and still contains the books, wood carvings and furniture of the Browne family, whose home it was for over four centuries.

In contrast Brockhole is a much grander gentleman's mansion. Designed by Daniel Gibson, it was built at the turn of the century for a silk merchant at a time when wealthy businessmen, unhindered by planning permission, were establishing their smart residences along the banks of Windermere. Now much of the remaining shoreline is owned by the National Trust and is thus protected from further development. In 1966 the house, which was being used as a nursing home, was bought by the Lake District National Park and three years later it became the country's first National Park Visitor Centre.

Until recently Brockhole was the headquarters of the National Park, but

Town End

this has now moved to Murley Moss at Kendal, hopefully leaving more room at Brockhole for the primary purpose of informing visitors. As well as a gift shop and restaurant there are regular exhibitions, slide shows and displays. With pleasant gardens and grounds reaching down to the shores of Windermere and an adventure playground, as well as its indoor attractions, Brockhole provides an introduction to the Lakes, though before planning a visit it is a good idea to consult the Events Diary.

We returned to find our car virtually alone on the car park, and much relieved that the windows were still intact, began to take off our boots and waterproofs. It was then that we noticed the mudflap lying on the ground. Further inspection revealed a dent in the door and also in the wing. In an empty car park, and with enough space to manoeuvre an army, someone had still managed to hit us.

But as we drove home our spirits soon lifted for already we were planning another visit, a backpack round the fells. Next time we would carry our belongings with us. Next time there would be no problems.

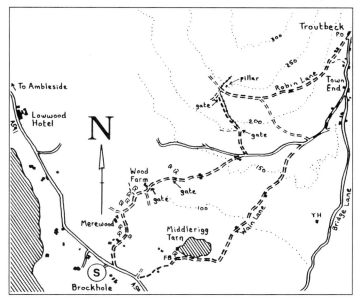

6.3

ROUTE DESCRIPTION

Troutbeck (*Trout stream*)

From Brockhole turn right along the main road, then take the bridleway up Mirk Lane which is almost opposite. The track bends right in front of Merewood Lodge, then climbs the hill and the noise of the traffic is soon left behind. Keep right at the fork into Newclose Wood, where the track is banked with bluebells, then meeting a farm road you pass the whitewashed Wood Farm with its round Westmorland chimney, a style of which Wordsworth was very fond.

The bridleway climbs on past a huge ancient sycamore and reaching some old barns Middlerigg Tarn appears to the right with Windermere beyond. Joining Holbeck Lane by Castle Syke Farm, go right and then left up the footpath opposite, a gated walled track which climbs past fields bouncing with lambs in the spring.

Passing Martin's Wood a track is joined at a stile by a gate and then you turn right along Robin Lane. Immediately opposite is a step stile in the wall, which leads up to a ruined stone pillar. This was built on the site of one of

129

Father West's Stations, viewpoints which he selected for tourists and described in his famous eighteenth century *Guide to the Lakes*. In those days Robin Lane would have been an important thoroughfare and the position was chosen for its extensive view of Windermere.

When the lane forks by a seat, keep straight on, and follow the main track down past the cottages to Troutbeck Post Office, where if you are lucky they may be serving cups of tea and coffee. Troutbeck is little more than a series of hamlets strung out along the road, each clustered around its own well, with the church down by the river and the Mortal Man Inn, at the northern end of the village, ¹/₂ mile away.

Town End

Turn right along the road past the houses to Town End, which has a very fine bank barn opposite. This house, which was enlarged in the seventeenth century, was the home of the Browne family for over 400 years. The last George Browne had three daughters, none of whom married, and in 1947 the property passed to the National Trust. It is, without doubt, the finest example of a Cumbrian statesman's house and, assisted by the warmth of an open fire and the welcome, feels very much a home.

Middlerigg Tarn (*Middle ridge tarn*)

Take the higher road towards Ambleside, then after the layby, turn left down Wain Lane. The bridleway descends to pass Middlerigg Tarn, and even though it is private, there is a good view of this artificial tarn with its fringe of bulrushes, little island, and small stream, while at the water's edge by the dam stand the mansion and a large boathouse.

Crossing a little clapperbridge by a ford, continue to the main road where you turn right back to Brockhole. The house was built in 1899 for William Henry Gaddum, a name implying rather frivolous tendencies, but he was a wealthy Manchester businessman, and the gardens are unchanged from when they were first laid out by Thomas Mawson.

WALK 6.4: DUBBS RESERVOIR TO HOLEHIRD

Tarns:	Dubbs Reservoir
	Holehird Tarn
Distance:	5¹/₂ miles
Ascent:	550ft
Summary:	Easy walking with superb views to a beautiful garden. (Donation requested)

NOTE - Dogs must be on a lead on the Holehird Estate and NO DOGS PLEASE in the gardens.

Starting Point: (GR 425006) 2 miles north of Windermere on the minor road from Troutbeck to Ings. Space for a few cars at the end of Dubbs Road.

Alternative Start: (GR 408005) For garden visitors only.

Its surface spread with yellow and white water-lilies, and surrounded by wild irises and almost luminous marsh marigolds, Holehird Tarn looks enchanting. Trees bend protectively over the edge, white fronted coots bustle to and fro, while patrolling the still waters is a stately swan.

On our last visit we met a lady who told us about the swans. "They've got some cygnets" she said. "I've been coming up here every afternoon and the eggs have taken 38 days to hatch. I hope the parents are more responsible than they were last year." Last year the tarn had been dredged by the anglers and with provisions running low the male swan had decided to move his family. Off they set towards Windermere, the three cygnets sitting on the pen's back. When they came to the main road, with its usual continuous stream of vehicles, the cob circled protectively, hissing at anyone who came too near. A car stopped, the driver got out and held up the traffic for them to cross. It was a lovely, peaceful, rural Lakeland scene, but surprisingly some motorists were annoyed at the delay.

Like many lowland tarns Holehird is not natural, but is the result of William Groves damming the beck in 1902 to provide an ornamental pond for his mansion. Now used by fishermen who catch roach and perch and the occasional large carp, the tarn lies within the Holehird Estate at Troutbeck Bridge.

With its large house, formal and informal gardens, farms, cottages and woodland, Holehird is a most impressive place and has all the air of a stately home. The Mansion House, which was considerably enlarged in the nineteenth century by John Dunlop, a Manchester industrialist, and still further in the early 1900s by the Groves family, is now a Leonard Cheshire Home, and the estate is administered by Cumbria County Council.

The real glory of Holehird, though, is its surroundings. Both the Dunlops and the Groves were enthusiastic gardeners and Mr Groves was a sponsor of the famous plant hunting expeditions of Reginald Farrer and William Purdom. But after the 1939-45 war the grounds began to fall into decay. Rescued with the formation of the Lakeland Horticultural Society, throughout the year the borders, rockery and greenhouses are now busy with gardeners hard at work. Almost all are unpaid volunteers, drawn from the Society's 1500 members, and the garden is the home of the National Collections of Astilbe, Hydrangea and Polystichum. One of the finest times for a visit is

Holehird Tarn

when the rhododendrons and azaleas are in bloom, and a walk in early summer through the brilliant colours and scents should not be missed.

ROUTE DESCRIPTION

Dubbs Reservoir (*Deep pool reservoir*)

Dubbs Road is classified as a bridleway and the unsurfaced track leads between stone walls past green fields grazed by suckler cows. The grassy verges are covered with flowers, and as well as the more common varieties there are the delicate nodding pink bells of water avens and the dark blue spikes of bugle, a narcotic which in medieval times was used as a cure-all for many ailments.

After nearly a mile of easy walking along the quiet track, with the only disturbance the occasional fisherman's car, the grassy dam is reached. The surroundings, studded with notices, are rather forbidding, and though access may be restricted for safety reasons, the nesting swans were ignoring the warnings about anglers casting. The reservoir, which belongs to North West Water, was originally built to supply Windermere, but is now used only as a supplement to the Thirlmere Aqueduct. It is a rather boring stretch of water, and looks very artificial for the dam is lined with railings, so turning your back on it, press on up the track.

Garburn Road (*Road by the stream in the strip of land*)

As Dubbs Road climbs the hill the reservoir looks better in retrospect. Ahead lies Wansfell, to the right are the steep slopes of Sour Hows, and the lush roadside vegetation has been replaced by yellow tormentil, the lacy white heads of pignut, and brilliant blue germander speedwell. Below in the valley is the long, straggling village of Troutbeck, then as you round the corner the view is of the mountains. The pink scoop of Red Screes dominates and beyond the dip of the Kirkstone Pass rises Caudale Moor with Thornthwaite Beacon on the skyline, while above the plantation is the switchback ridge of the Kentmere Fells.

A footpath downhill cuts off the acute bend in the track, but it is easier to continue past the plantation to the Garburn Road and then hairpin back. The track is still classified as a public road, but though we have some sympathy for motorcyclists, we had none for the people in their 4x4.

The green hill in the centre of the valley is Troutbeck Tongue, and crouching low in front is the whitewashed sheep farm of Troutbeck Park. The estate, which dates back to medieval times, was bought by Beatrix Potter in 1924 and given to the National Trust on her death. Her book *The Fairy Caravan* is set in this area and has drawings of the farm.

The track goes gently downhill, and in the valley bottom is Limefitt Park, where they have planted over 1500 trees. This large camping and caravan park won the AA's campsite of the year award in 1992. Keeping to the upper road to pass beneath Whiteside Plantation, you can just make out the top of Troutbeck's eighteenth-century church tower.

Holehird (*Hird's Holding*)

Meeting the tarmac road you turn right, and then fork left downhill at the junction. The hill above is Allen Knotts, the site of an Iron Age fort, while beside the road the grassy banks are brilliant in early June with the wood cranesbill and the large bright yellow petals of the Welsh poppy. There are ferns in abundance, including the more unusual scaly male fern *Dryopteris pseudomas* whose stems are covered by a dense reddish brown fur.

Turn left again on the tarmac lane and past the houses, where a marvellous panorama appears across Windermere to the Langdale Pikes, and Holehird Tarn can be seen below. A gate leads down into the Holehird Estate (all dogs on leads please) and passing the cottages and the old stable block, take the left fork just before the Mansion House. The house, which is now leased to the Leonard Cheshire Foundation, was built in 1854 and Beatrix Potter twice stayed here with her parents for their summer holidays.

Following the tarmac track past a grass bank which has been developed as a spring meadow, the Lakeland Horticultural Society Gardens are reached. The society was formed in 1969 when it took over the garden, which had become neglected, and the outstanding result is a wide variety of trees, shrubs, herbaceous perennials, alpines and bulbs. Though all the work is voluntary, costs must be met and a donation is requested from visitors who are welcome to look round. An excellent booklet is on sale, but please note dogs are not allowed in the gardens.

Holehird Tarn

The tarmac drive leads down across the park and through a stone gateway nearly to the road, where a little footpath turns off through the trees to the tarn. Following the narrow path which threads between the rhododendrons, walk round the tarn in a clockwise direction. The little island at the far end is used as a nesting place by the swans.

After the small boathouse, the path continues round the tarn and a return can be made up the main drive, but if you are visiting the gardens, take the path across the field to a stone belvedere, then make your way through the formal gardens and by the ponds.

Orrest (*Battle*)

Retracing your steps past the stable block to leave the grounds of Holehird, the footpath is rejoined and you turn right to follow the tarmac lane to Far Orrest. Go through the kissing gate on the footpath to Garburn via Near Orrest, then keeping to the left of the buildings, waymarks guide you on a complicated route round the farm, crossing an old walled lane, through the

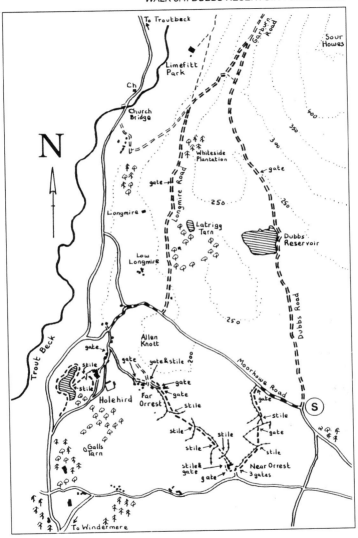

6.4

fields to the left of the white cottage, and then across another old walled lane.

The footpath across the fields is well supplied with stiles and over to the right you can see the gentle pyramid of Orrest Head, a famous viewpoint and a popular walk from Windermere. Orrest means battle, but which battle is unknown, though it has been the centre of a recent confrontation between Wainwright devotees who wanted to erect a memorial, and the Planning Board who refused permission.

Approaching Near Orrest, a step stile outlined in white paint indicates the way, and you go round to the right and across the front of the house. Three closely spaced gates lead into the fields again, and the wall is followed along the edge to a ladder stile. Cross the next field diagonally to the left-most gate, then after the ladder stile beyond, the wall is followed leftwards to Moorhowe Road. The start of the walk is then 300 yards up the road to the right.

7: Kentmere and Longsleddale Tarns

WALK 7.1: KENTMERE TARN

Tarns:	Kentmere Tarn
Distance:	5 miles
Ascent:	550ft
Summary:	Easy walking on good tracks in a quiet valley.
Starting Point:	(GR 456043) Kentmere village. Parking by church, but this fills up very quickly, especially at weekends.
Alternative Start:	(GR 456020) Very limited roadside parking near factory.

Kentmere Tarn has had an exciting life. First it was there, then it wasn't, and now it has appeared again. Once a shallow lake filled the Kentmere valley below St Cuthbert's church, and in the clear water flourished tiny algae called diatoms whose skeletons are made of silicon. When these microscopic creatures died, they formed a sediment on the bed of the tarn. Gradually the water silted up and finally, around 1840, the tarn was drained when the River Kent was deepened to improve the grazing in the valley. Though the land reclamation was not very successful, and the resulting marsh became overgrown with rush and sedge, Harriet Martineau wrote in 1854 that you "will look for Kentmere Tarn, and wonder to see no trace of it. It is drained away; and fertile fields now occupy the place of the swamp, reeds and shallow water".

In the 1930s the Cape Asbestos Company began to mine the bed of this ancient mere. There was an aerial ropeway with a chain of buckets and the black sludge dredged from the bottom of the tarn was dried and the diatomite extracted. After grinding it to a powder the silica was mixed with asbestos to make soundproof boarding and insulated bricks.

On finishing our walk we called at our favourite tea shop in Staveley, where as usual we chatted to the two ladies who run the cafe. "Kentmere Tarn" said one of them. "I used to be a secretary at the factory and my brother-in-law worked on the dredging". Then she went on to tell us how in 1955 he had discovered, preserved in the mud on the bottom of the tarn, an old wooden boat which was dated to the tenth century. Two of these ancient Viking dugout canoes have been found. One is in the National Maritime Museum in London and the other in the museum at Kendal.

In 1971 the factory turned to other materials and the excavations came to an end. Kentmere's unique claim to industrial fame, the only diatomite mine in England, was no more. But in the place where the diatomite deposits had been, now lay a new tarn. It may not be the original, but once again Kentmere has the mere after which the village is named.

ROUTE DESCRIPTION
Sawmill Cottage

Opposite the church a farm road leads westwards to Kentmere Hall, a farmhouse attached to a ruined fourteenth-century pele tower. The estate was given to Richard Gilpin in the reign of King John and was to remain the home of the Gilpins for over 200 years. Richard is reputed to have killed the last wild boar in the area, but Bernard was the most famous member of the family, revered as 'The Apostle of the North' for his good works in the sixteenth century. Gilpin is still a local name and there are several Gilpins in the churchyard.

Going through the second gate opposite the farm the bridleway climbs above the trees of Hall Wood and past an old quarry. The gated track, its grassy banks covered in violets, climbs steadily with expanding views of the Kentmere valley, and rounding the rocky Whiteside End, which at 951 ft is the

Kentmere Hall

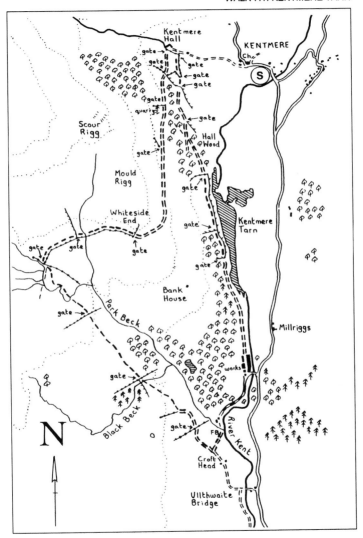

7.1

highest point of the walk, continues towards the bumpy top of Applethwaite Common.

It is a gentle descent by the wall to Park Beck, but don't cross the stream; turn left over the moor to ford it a little way downstream where there is a mass of wild daffodils. Continuing downhill you can see, to the right of the Kentmere valley, the monument on High Knott which was built in 1803 in memory of Thomas Williamson by his son. After passing Meadowplatts Plantation and crossing Black Beck by a ruined stone hut, the gated track becomes enclosed by walls. Turn left at the track junction and go over the footbridge past Sawmill Cottage, now a pottery, which stands at the confluence of Black Beck and the River Kent. The mill, which was built about the same time that the mere was drained, provided timber for the new Windermere Railway.

Kentmere Tarn

Passing a bluebell wood the tarmac drive leads beside the River Kent, then at Waterford Bridge you turn left through the works. Fringed with scrub woodland, the track leads past Kentmere Tarn, where a bollard and a concrete base beside the water are all that remain of the aerial ropeway which carried a chain of buckets from the excavator to the factory. The long narrow tarn, here merely a widening in the River Kent, seems more like a canal, but further on an isthmus of land separates the broadened river from an almost separate tarn and beyond is the village of Kentmere. The reclaimed tarn is now a private fishery with several small boats and platforms for the fishermen.

Entering Hall Wood, keep to the lower track then walk back through the field to Kentmere Hall where you turn right to return to St Cuthbert's church. The simple rendered building, which was restored in 1866, contains a memorial to Bernard Gilpin and from the porch is a view of Kentmere Tarn.

WALK 7.2: SKEGGLES WATER

Tarn:	Skeggles Water
Distance:	6 miles
Ascent:	900ft
Summary:	Old drove roads link to give easy walking round a lonely tarn.
Starting Point:	(GR 484057) Sadgill at the head of Longsleddale. Parking for about a dozen cars at the road end.

Hound trails are usually jolly affairs; crowds of people and dogs, and lots of noise. Lots and lots of noise, as with one great leap the hounds clear the final wall and race neck and neck to the finish, amid the cheers and shouts of the onlookers.

Longsleddale was different. For a start there were only three hounds. They looked keen enough, yet as the dogs stood beside their owners there was an air of uncertainty as if all this was a bit new. Noses sniffed the air and necks strained at leashes, but it was still two months to the start of the season and indeed it was a practice, a trial run for young dogs yet to race in earnest. Hound trailing as a sport is controlled by a ruling body, set up in 1906 to put an end to the widespread practice of swapping dogs, for then, as now, much of the appeal of the sport was in the betting. A trail of around 10 miles, made by dragging a paraffin and aniseed soaked rag over the fells, takes the dogs a mere half an hour. In May, when foxhunting finishes, the trailing season starts and runs through until October, but this was a cold, grey day in February.

Well Foot Farm

At least it was cold and grey in the valley. But after a short climb, we came out onto the moor of Cocklaw Fell to find that it was a perfect day on the tops. Brilliant blue sky, warm sunshine, and a view that stretched clear and sharp right across Lakeland to the far distant summits of the Scafells, and in the middle of the moor lay Skeggles Water.

Skeggles Water seems to be a no-man's land. Surrounded by public rights of way it sits like royalty amid the peaty moor, defying commoners to approach. It is unusual on Lakeland fells to find notices demanding that one keep to the path, but the tolerance that elsewhere has allowed walkers free rein over the fells is here in abeyance. Grouse moors perhaps or duck shooting? Or are they hoping to revive the long dead plan to mine for diatomite?

Longsleddale, which escaped the fate of becoming the route of the main railway line to Scotland, was also considered for the M6 and there was a plan to reopen the quarries, but fortunately it is still as described in Murray's nineteenth-century guide: "a genuine and lovely specimen of natural scenery". The valley is one of the very few sites in the Lakes where the bird's-eye primrose may be found, and the woodland is noted for the wild cherry and the bird cherry, both trees a mass of blossom in the spring.

On the fell tops the sun still shone, while below us the valley was filled with a white fog, and as we slowly descended the cold damp closed about us. In Longsleddale everyone still thought it a bad day, but we and the hounds knew better.

ROUTE DESCRIPTION

Skeggles Water (*Skakel's lake*)

From the little humpback bridge at the end of the valley, the byway to Kentmere leads left past Low Sadgill Farm. The walled lane, an old drove road, climbs to a second gate, then leaving the main track you turn left to cross a stream and follow the path as it contours round the hillside. Below in the extended narrow valley of Longsleddale is the River Sprint, whose name does indeed mean fast, for the athletic 'sprinter' has the same Norse derivation.

After going through the next gate few signs of the right of way remain, but climbing the rough grassy fellside, a gate is reached in the top corner. Continuing across Cocklaw Fell, whose name probably refers to the mating dance of the black grouse, the path soon becomes more definite and Skeggles Water comes into view. This remote tarn is surprisingly large, but there is no public access to its rather boggy shoreline. Grassy fields edge the western rim, but to the east lies heather moor where new ditches have been dug to drain the land. The peaty area around the tarn was once cut for fuel, and like the neighbouring Kentmere Tarn, Skeggles Water was considered for diatomite extraction, but luckily the scheme never materialised.

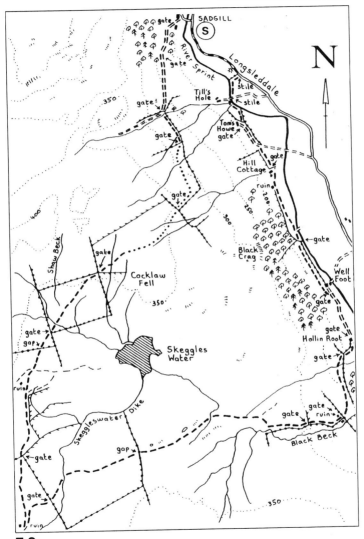

7.2

The route continues through the gates over rough grassland, brightened in the wetter places by the pretty pink ragged robin and the golden stars of bog asphodel, then approaching a ruin on Green Quarter Fell, which is named after the hamlet in the Kentmere valley, the path divides. Keep to the left and follow the new fence to another gate.

The path now begins to descend gently, but at a cairned junction by a ruined building, take the path which bends sharply back left to climb for a short way to a gate in the wall. A waymarked little path sets off through the heather to cross Skeggleswater Dike, the outflow from the tarn which has recently been enlarged with the help of a JCB, then passing to the south of Skeggles Water it goes through a gap in a wall. After about ¹/₂ mile, the path makes a sharp right turn and another wall is followed down to a kissing gate.

Longsleddale (*Long valley*)

Reaching the derelict buildings of Hollin Root, the old drove road up the Longsleddale valley is joined. In 1735 this was known as the "high road from Ambleside to Appleby". Hollin refers to holly trees and the clippings were once used as winter feed for the sheep, who surprisingly seem to have enjoyed them.

Above Well Foot the bridleway has been diverted into the field, then passing the ruins of Underhill House and beneath Hill Cottage, it continues up the long glacial valley following the River Sprint. Nearing Tom's Howe, when the track bends up towards the farm, go through the gate into the field, where a grassy path joins the river again. Cross the bridge which serves Till's Hole, then a footpath goes through a kissing gate and across the field to the road. Stockdale Farm, on the hillside above, now a Craft Centre, is famed for having given the geological name to the bed of Silurian Shale upon which it stands. To the left is the conical mound of Whirl Howe, an ancient Bronze Age burial mound, then it is only about ¹/₄ mile back along the tarmac to the road end and the little packhorse bridge.

WALK 7.3: POTTER FELL

Tarns:	Ghyll Pool
	Potter Tarn
	Gurnal Dubs (Fothergill Tarn)
	Low Taggleshaw
Distance:	7 miles
Ascent:	850ft
Summary:	Easy paths lead by the River Kent and up onto Potter Fell.
Starting Point:	(GR 504957) Burneside. Works car park opposite the church.

The River Kent at Cowen Head Mill

Potter Fell is an inviting name suggesting gentle fell walks, not too strenuous and with an air of peace and tranquillity. A suitable outing for an easy day. And the tarns of Potter Fell will not disappoint, for between the main A591, with its continuous stream of traffic, and the infinitely quieter valley of Longsleddale, is a hillside half asleep in the sunshine. But it wasn't always so.

The tarns owe their origin to paper, for in order to supply his mills at Cowen Head and Burneside with a steady, high pressure supply of water, James Cropper turned the natural shallow pools on Potter Fell into reservoirs. The date was around 1900, but the history of paper-making on the banks of the River Kent goes back much further than this.

One of the surprises about the eighteenth and nineteenth centuries in the Lake District is the industry. There were mines and quarries back to Elizabethan times and even earlier, but perhaps less obvious is that while William and Dorothy Wordsworth were living and writing of their rural idyll at Dove Cottage, with never a mention of the mills, industry was growing fast. During the early 1800s the valley of the River Kent was more heavily industrialised than even Birmingham, with a mill for every 315 people living in the valley, more than four times the density achieved by the capital of the Midlands.

To Dorothy, Thomas Ashburner was the neighbour who lived with his family in a small cottage opposite, but fifty years earlier in the valley of the River Kent, the name Thomas Ashburner meant paper-making. Buying Cowen Head Mill for £130, this Kendal bookseller turned what had been a fulling mill into a paper mill. Paper in those days was made one sheet at a time using flax and hemp, and mechanisation did not begin until 1833 when one of the first Fourdrinier paper making machines was introduced. Then, in 1845, along came the founder of the Cropper dynasty.

James Cropper, a Quaker, became fascinated with paper-making when at Edinburgh University, and through his uncle, who owned the mills at Burneside, he came with his new wife to Cowen Head. The mills prospered, the Cropper family prospered, and so did their workers, for James and his partner John Bryce, with themselves as teachers, started evening classes in reading and writing for their illiterate employees. Mrs Bryce, inspired by Bournville, was responsible for the building of workers' houses in the Ivy Cottage Estate, and James Cropper was one of the founders of Kendal Hospital.

The Kent still supplies the works at Burneside, and there was certainly plenty of water as we followed the tree-lined river upstream. At Bowston the mill pool reflects the cottages and at Cowen Head the river flows in a delightful gorge spanned by a high arched bridge, while along the river banks are marsh marigolds, yellow monkey-flower and the dainty water forget-me-not.

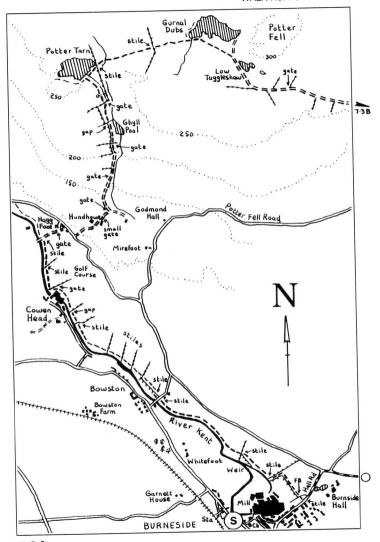

7.3A

It is now a long time since the valley of the River Kent rivalled Birmingham. Bowston Mill has gone while Cowen Head Mill has been converted into flats, but on Potter Fell the tarns still supply water, Burneside still produces paper, and after five generations, a century and a half later, the company chairman is still a Cropper, and his name is still James.

ROUTE DESCRIPTION

Bowston (*Bolt's village*)

The road by St Oswald's church, in the centre of Burneside, leads over the River Kent and past James Cropper's works. Paper has been made here since 1833, and in 1995 the firm celebrated the 150th anniversary of the arrival of the first James Cropper at Burneside.

Joining the main road turn left, and then at the end of the houses a stile takes you onto the Dales Way, a long distance path from Ilkley to Bowness. Heading for Bowston, the footpath crosses a little footbridge and follows the fence round the perimeter of the factory.

A step stile leads into the field beside the leat that serves the mill, and the path keeps by the fence. Passing the weir, a rather grand ladder stile is reached, and the path cuts across a bend in the river before continuing upstream to the attractive two-arched stone bridge at Bowston.

Cowen Head

Leaving the Dales Way, which now follows the west bank of the river, turn right along the road for a few yards, and then left down the track and over a wooden step stile. The path keeps to the edge of the field, where ox-eye daisies flower in the summer, and past a weir which served the now demolished 1874 mill.

A series of ladder stiles leads beside the River Kent, and on the opposite bank is the route of the old railway line which connected Bowston Mill to Cowen Head. Originally built as a narrow gauge tramway, with two horses pulling trucks to the mill, it was relaid in 1927 as a railway using rails captured in Palestine from the Turks. The engine, which was named Rachael after the daughter of James W. Cropper, is now preserved at the Lakeside and Haverthwaite Railway.

At Cowen Head Mill the river flows through a deep rocky channel and the path squeezes round the end of a wall. This old paper mill was originally a fulling mill, and it was here that Thomas Ashburner started his paper-making business in 1746. The building has recently been restored and converted into "secluded luxury properties".

Ghyll Pool

The path skirts the mill buildings round the edge of an unexpected golf course, and continues past the weir and beside the river to a ramshackle private bridge. The Dales Way has been re-routed to the other side of the river to avoid this crossing. Joining a stone-walled track, which leads up to Hagg Foot Farm, go left through the yard and out to the road.

About 100 yards along the road to the right is the bridleway to Low Hundhowe Farm. Passing the farm and an ancient barn, go through the gate onto a narrow walled track, which soon leads to another gate where the footpath to Potter Tarn leaves the bridleway and goes left.

Climbing gradually, on the edge of the steep wooded slope of Emmanuel's Ghyll, which was carved by glacial melt water, the path comes out into the fields and past the concrete dam of Ghyll Pool. This small reservoir, which has grassy banks and is surrounded by a fence to keep stock out, was built in 1934 to supply water to James Cropper's paper mill at Burneside.

Potter Tarn (*Pasture by the deep pool*)

Further up the path is an overgrown pool, part of the water supply which the stream has been diverted to feed, and ahead is the ugly concrete dam of Potter Tarn. Though the tarn is a major water supply for James Cropper's works, the reservoir is now only half full as the level was considerably lowered around 1990 when the dam became unsafe.

Gurnal Dubs

The path crosses the stream beneath the slipway, where concrete blocks break up the water flow to prevent erosion of the stream bed, and then follows the dam wall to a stile on the right. Continue along a raised earth bank and over the beck to climb the bracken covered hillside to a ladder stile, which at nearly 1000ft is the highest point of the walk. Beyond Potter Tarn to the west you can see Middle Fairbank Reservoir, flanked in the distance by Black Combe and the Coniston Fells. Having picked these out the eye travels on to the dip of the Wrynose Pass, the bumpy top of Crinkle Crags and the steep drop of Mickledore which divides Sca Fell and Scafell Pike.

Now descending gradually, the path comes to Gurnal Dubs, where heather moorland encroaches on the banks of the tarn. There is a grand boathouse, restored in 1986, complete with chimney, and also a wooded island. Much more attractive than Potter Tarn, it was formed from two smaller ice scoured natural tarns, and is fished by the Kent Angling Association.

Low Taggleshaw

The path crosses the outflow which feeds Ghyll Pool, and going along the little stone-walled dam, continues through the heather to join a track. Turning right beside a fence, this is followed past the almost completely overgrown Low Taggleshaw, a small patch of water in the centre of a marsh. Wainwright has upset the landowner by describing the route to the other Taggleshaw tarns, but the usual Lakeland tolerance of walkers seems to be absent here

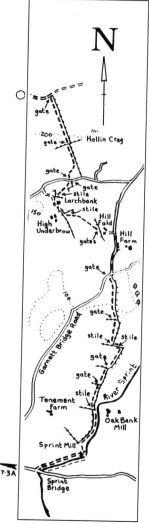

and access to them is now forbidden.

Burneside (*Brunulf's hillside*)

The track swings left, heading towards the distant pleated folds of the Howgill Fells, while to the south lies Kendal, surrounded by a patchwork of green fields. Follow the gated track for about ½ mile, then just after the bend turn right through a field gate and follow the wall downhill. These slate walls high on the fellside, which run in straight lines enclosing neat rectangles and squares, were built as a result of the nineteenth-century Enclosure Acts, while those down in the valley, which form a jigsaw of shapes, are much older.

The path curves round a knoll to a gate onto Potter Fell Road where you take the footpath opposite, which leads to a U-shaped stile on the right of the house. Joining the track to Larchbank, go past the whitewashed house and through a couple of gates, then head across the field and go through the yard of Hill Fold Farm.

Turn right on the lane and past Hill Farm to a T-junction, where if time is short, you can return to Burneside along Garnett Bridge Road. The footpath route via Sprint Bridge goes straight on by the field boundary, following a series of stiles along field edges to reach the River Sprint opposite Oak Bank Bobbin Mill. Built in the first half of the nineteenth century, this was one of many bobbin mills that were established to feed Lancashire's cotton trade. Oak Bank, which was still working in the 1960s, was one of the last mills to succumb.

The path then leads through the trees, by an old leat and past the huge pipes of the Thirlmere aqueduct to reach Sprint Mill. Though the site is medieval, the three-storied mill was built in 1825 to produce yarn for the hand-knitted stocking industry, and was later used as a bobbin mill and a saw mill.

The rightmost track leads out to the road at Sprint Bridge where you turn right past the ruins

7.3B

of Burneside Hall whose fourteenth-century pele tower sports a satellite dish. The attractive gatehouse was added a couple of centuries later, around the time when the poet Richard Braithwaite lived here. It is now only a short way, turning left at the junction, down Hall Road, back to the industrial village of Burneside.

WALK 7.4: KEMP TARN

Tarns:	Kemp Tarn
Distance:	1½ miles
Ascent:	500ft
Summary:	A short walk to a fell-top tarn.
Starting Point:	(GR 469986) Staveley. Roadside parking by the church.

Beside Kemp Tarn, the Warrior's Tarn, stood the warrior himself. He stared at us, we stared at him. "He doesn't look fierce" we said and circling warily past, attained the summit of Reston Scar. Behind us the bull gave a deep sigh and lay down on the grass.

Staveley used to be a bottleneck. Jammed with cars every weekend, with people impatient to get moving again, it was a place most people were glad to leave behind. But now the narrow main street has been bypassed, removing one more obstruction in the headlong dash for the Lakes, and Staveley has reverted to a quieter life.

The village was remembered with affection by Dorothy Wordsworth after the walking tour she undertook with her brother in 1794: "I am always glad

Above Kemp Tarn

to see Staveley; it is a place I dearly love to think of - the first mountain village that I came to with William when we first began our pilgrimage together".

We hadn't thought of Staveley as being among the mountains. But standing on the crest of Reston Scar, though it is just 837ft above sea level, we looked down the precipitous slopes that drop towards the tiny toy houses far below and felt, just for the moment, on top of the world.

ROUTE DESCRIPTION

Kemp Tarn (*Warrior's tarn*)

From St James's church follow Brow Lane to the War Memorial and turn left to Barley Bridge. Staveley was the centre of a thriving bobbin manufacturing industry in the eighteenth century and this was the site of the largest of its five bobbin mills. There was also a seventeenth-century corn mill, but both the water-wheels have gone and now only the weir remains.

Opposite the bridge a track leads uphill and going through a gate on the left, continues up between stone walls. The edge of a field is then followed and crossing the bottom of the garden of Sunnybank a track is joined which climbs past an underground reservoir. The grassy mound is completely covered in summer by ox-eye daisies, and the juice from the stems of these attractive flowers was once used as eye drops.

The track continues through the higher of two gates, then zigzags up the little rocky fell to a wall corner. Going through the leftmost gate, Kemp Tarn lies on the fell-top over to the right, edged with bogbean, rushes and lesser spearwort and from the tarn you can look north-east across the Kentmere valley into Longsleddale. The owners of the Staveley tea shop told us that they skated on Kemp Tarn when they were children.

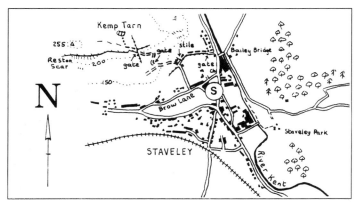

7.4

The track fizzles out on the fell top near the cairn on the summit of Reston Scar (837ft) which on our visit was surrounded by reclining cows and a docile bull. The large expanse of water on the far side of the busy A591 is Middle Fairbank Reservoir, while to the west lie Windermere, the Coniston Fells and the Langdale Pikes.

Staveley (*Wood where staves are obtained*)

Retrace your steps to the gate and down the track, where the houses of Staveley appear below framed by the V-shaped hillside. Follow the track downhill by a tiny stream, where you can find the pale blue flowers of water forget-me-not, and also the brighter blue brooklime. Brooklime, whose Latin name *Veronica beccabunga* is easily remembered as it bungs up becks, has edible leaves and was once used as a cure for scurvy. Passing the reservoir, keep straight on by Sunnybank and down the tarmac lane. Turn left along the road, past the school, and back to the slate church with its neat little spire. St James's church is modern and replaced the Chapel of St Margaret at Over Staveley, of which only the fourteenth-century tower remains.

WALK 7.5: YOKE TO KENTMERE RESERVOIR

Tarns: Kentmere Reservoir
                       Rainsborrow Tarn

Distance: 11 miles

Ascent: 2850ft

Summary: A hidden tarn on the switchback ridge to Froswick, with a return by the source of the River Kent to a quiet reservoir.

Starting Point: (GR 456043) Kentmere village. Limited parking by church.

High on the Kentmere Fells, where the shoulder of the grassy summit of Yoke ends in the steep cliffs of Rainsborrow Crag, lies an unnamed and secret tarn. This is a place known only to a few, for although there is seldom a day when no-one traverses the switchback ridge of Froswick, Ill Bell and Yoke, that trio of summits on the ever popular Kentmere Horseshoe, probably less than one in a thousand ever turns aside to seek out this little tarn.

We very nearly didn't find it ourselves. The book was almost complete. For over three years we had been searching the fells, visiting all the tiny specks of blue recorded on the map to see if they were tarns, and only a handful remained. "It's very small" we said, "hardly worth a visit", but just to be sure one June afternoon, we traversed the Kentmere tops and strolled out to the commanding position on the edge of the crags.

The Kentmere Valley

"I've never seen anyone so surprised by a tarn" said our friend Val. Perched on the very end of the spur, and hidden until the last moment, lay a long dark pool. A lovely shining stretch of water with silver ripples, but was it a tarn? Our companions were adamant. "Of course it's a tarn" they said, "it's beautiful". To the north the view takes in the buttresses of Ill Bell and Froswick with beyond them the precipitous slopes that ring the head of the Kentmere valley, eastwards lie the lower moorlike summits of the Shap Fells, while far below in the valley is Kentmere Reservoir.

There is no secret, though, about Kentmere Reservoir, almost a small lake in size, but for some strange reason its status is in doubt. Like an errant relative of whose activities the rest of the family disapproves, it is 'not talked about' when the subject is tarns. True, it is artificial, built in the mid-nineteenth century to regulate the River Kent for the mills that depended on its steady flow, but many such stretches of water, several of them of far later date, and even small fishing ponds, have been allotted formal recognition as tarns.

It had been a cold day on the tops and apart from a solitary cyclist who pedalled his way up to Thornthwaite Crag we had seen no sign of anyone all day, but as we walked slowly down the Nan Bield Pass we came upon a family group. Grazing peacefully on the rough grass were a shaggy-maned stallion, a mare and an unsteady foal, who looked up enquiringly as we passed. Semi-wild ponies such as these, black, brown and bay, roam the fells as far as Pooley Bridge.

Though now looking eminently respectable, and the subject of much discussion about how best to preserve its tranquillity by banning cars, Kentmere village once too was wild. The Low Bridge Inn, now a private house, was the first pub in England to lose its licence. Of course they blamed it on off-comers, but at the time it was alleged that it wasn't only the navvies building the reservoir who were permanently drunk.

ROUTE DESCRIPTION

Garburn Pass *(Pass by the stream in the strip of land)*

From Kentmere's restored sixteenth-century church, follow the tarmac lane which heads for the Garburn Pass, past the gated road to Hartrigg Farm. At the road end the bridleway to Troutbeck, an old packhorse way, ascends purposefully between stone walls while to the left you can see Kentmere Hall with its fourteenth-century castellated pele tower, and Kentmere Tarn beyond.

Rainsborrow Tarn *(Ravens' hill tarn)*

The stony track, on whose banks grow parsley fern and male fern, as well as the colourful foxglove, harebell and tormentil, continues to climb, and after a mile the top of the pass is reached. Geologists will tell you that the rocks here are the narrow outcropping band of Coniston Limestone which runs

155

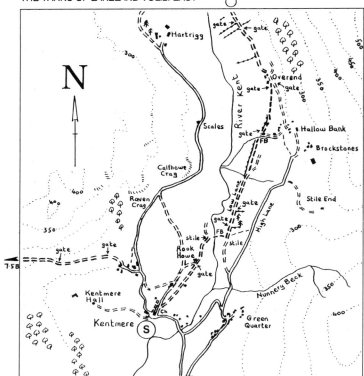

7.5A

right across the Lake District, but it is not very obvious to the untrained eye.

Go through the gate, then turn right and follow the wall along the ridge. The moor, which is rather boggy at first, is brightened by cotton-grass, while down to the left is the long green valley of Trout Beck. After another mile the path crosses a ladder stile at the wall corner and from here there is a very good view of Windermere.

The main route, which is heading for the summit of Yoke, must now be abandoned to contour across the pathless grassy slope to join a ruined wall. The tumbled stones are followed for ¹/₂ mile along the fellside, passing infant streams rising in the grass, until the cliff edge is reached, where steep and craggy slopes drop to Kentmere Reservoir and the disused slate quarry

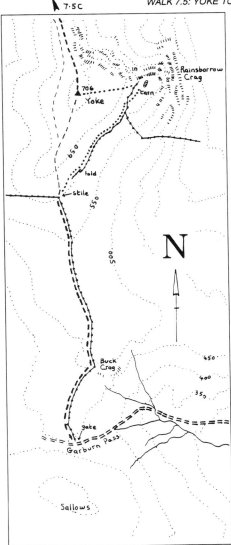

7·5C

below. The little tarn is then only a few steps to the right, on the summit of Rainsborrow Crag. Retained on a grassy shelf by a rocky rim, it is just about deep enough for a swim, and though a good 50 yards long, being out of sight from the main path and not mentioned by Wainwright, there are no cairns, and it sees few visitors.

Yoke

Returning to the wall and heading uphill by an old fence, steep pathless grassy slopes lead to the summit of Yoke (2316ft) whose cairn crowns a rocky knoll on the flat grassy top. To the west lies Red Screes and beyond the still active Pets Quarry rises the bump of Great Gable. Further west are the Scafells and further still the Coniston Fells, while ahead the broad ridge path continues over the summit of Ill Bell.

Ill Bell (*steep hill*)

There is an easy descent to a grassy col, then a straightforward

7.5B

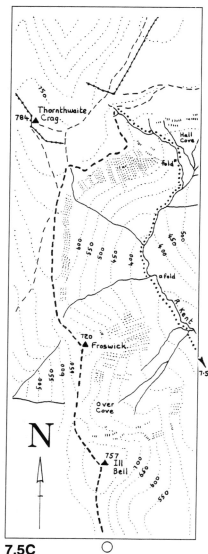

climb up the grassy ridge. Two fine cairns mark the summit at 2483ft, but a subsidiary cairn overlooking the Troutbeck valley was destroyed in the summer of 1994 by vandals claiming that piles of stones on mountains are environmentally unacceptable because they are man-made. "This", said Wainwright, "is one of the most distinctive summits in Lakeland".

Froswick

After a stony descent to the north-west to skirt the edge of Over Cove, and another steep pull up, the compact summit of Froswick (2362ft) is reached. From the cairn you look down into the Kentmere valley and there is a splendid view of Kentmere Reservoir.

Hall Cove

Thornthwaite Beacon, the prominent stone column on the skyline, disappears from sight as the path dips to the col, and to the left Scot Rake slants down to the Troutbeck valley. This ancient trackway, which was the route followed by the Roman road of High Street on its descent to Ambleside, was also the way raiders from Scotland came to steal cattle and sheep.

Climbing again, in ½ mile the path forks by a fence straining post embedded in a rock. Stay by the edge and

7.5C
158

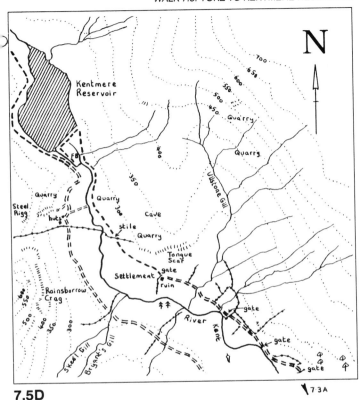

7.5D

7·3A

follow the narrow path past a stony gully, which is rather too steep for a comfortable descent into the Kentmere valley, but after nearly a mile the path makes a sharp right-angle turn round another scree gully, and this provides a much easier way down. This is the source of the River Kent, and on the damp gravel grows the delicate starry saxifrage *Saxifraga stellaris* whose five small white petals are dotted at the base with two tiny yellow spots.

With the grassy nose of Lingmell End ahead, follow the gully down by the stony prow of Gavel Crag and into Hall Cove. It is a delightful secluded spot, and its large sheepfold was the site of our first mountain camp when one October night we and our two children crammed into a small orange ridge tent.

159

Kentmere Reservoir

It is an easy mile descending by the infant River Kent, but though the waterfalls are very attractive, few walkers come this way and there is no path. The growing river passes a strangely shaped sheepfold, near the site of an ancient settlement, and finally tumbles over the rocks to enter Kentmere Reservoir by a solitary larch tree.

Keeping to the right, a good path is joined which leads above the reservoir and past the dam, then a footbridge over the outflow joins the path on the far side of the valley. At the bottom of the grass covered dam, speckled with the small lupin-like leaves of lady's mantle, is a neat stone archway from which the River Kent emerges to hurry off down the valley. The setting is very dramatic, with steep slopes all round, while to the west Ill Bell forms a perfect pyramid. The little bump at the lowest point on the skyline is the shelter on the top of the Nan Bield Pass, once the main route to Shap, and you may be lucky enough to see the fell ponies which often graze on the lower slopes of Lingmell End.

Though the reservoir still manages to look a newcomer, it was built in 1848, a surprisingly long time ago, to maintain a constant flow of water to the mills along the river. This must have been successful for as Harriet Martineau observed, "the flow of water no longer fails". However the inhabitants of the farms and houses, who used the river as their water supply, were less happy and a raised embankment, which you can still see, was built to divert Lingmell Gill around the dam to ensure the flow down the valley.

Hallow Bank Quarter

On the far side of the dam a narrow trod leads above the wall and by the river past an old quarry where green slate was mined. The workings are quite extensive, with a water-filled level and a long, unsafe tunnel disappearing into the darkness. On the far side of the valley is another disused slate quarry beneath Steel Rigg, whose restored buildings now belong to Lancashire County Council, and the whitewashed Reservoir Cottage is used as a hostel.

After a ladder stile the path goes past the site of an ancient settlement dating back to Roman times. With circular stone-based huts and irregularly shaped stock pens, the farmstead was almost large enough to have been a village.

After the ruined Tongue House, the gated track continues down the valley through fields golden with marsh marigolds in spring, to meet the river by a little packhorse bridge. The Kent, which served over 90 mills, is reputed to be the swiftest flowing river in the country for it falls 1000ft in 25 miles. Reaching the farm at Overend, keep right along the gated bridleway, then joining a good track the stream is crossed below Hallow Bank at a bridge made of a single slab of slate. Such bridges are called 'clapper' bridges and are one of the earliest forms known.

Accompanied at first by a wall, Low Lane becomes enclosed after crossing another stream, and passes a little wood. At the highest point of the lane, under the power lines, a step stile leads over the wall, then a footpath crosses the field, past a cleft boulder, to a footbridge òver the river. Joining a walled track turn left past Rook Howe and take the lower track back into Kentmere where it joins the road by the church.

WALK 8.1 TARN HOWS

Tarns:	Wharton Tarn (High Cross Tarn)
	Rose Castle Tarn
	High Arnside Tarn
	Tarn Hows
Distance:	4 miles
Ascent:	350ft
Summary:	Though the circuit of Tarn Hows is a very popular walk the crowds are soon left behind to follow quiet paths through fields and woodland.
Starting Point:	(GR 326996) Tarn Hows, 3 miles north-west of Hawkshead. Car park.

As the group reached us, they stopped. It was a crisis. "It's muddy!" announced the lady, looking with disgust at the puddle, fully an inch in depth, which barred her way, "we'll have to go back", and turning round they walked slowly back up the path towards the car park. Well, it's one way of keeping Tarn Hows from being overrun, as with three-quarters of a million visitors every year it's a miracle the tarn has survived. Yet the National Trust has managed to preserve this idyllic picture-postcard scene. But it is not a new problem.

"A general habit of gramaphoning and wirelessing would be a great nuisance", wrote Beatrix Potter in the 1930s to Bruce Thompson, the National Trust's new land agent. "I was displeased one hot summer to see people going down from cars to the tarn." Mr Thompson had a hard act to follow for Beatrix, after initial reluctance, entered enthusiastically into the management of the Monk Coniston Estate. She had bought the estate in 1929 with the royalties of *The Tale of Little Pig Robinson* and *The Fairy Caravan* with the express intention of transferring half of it immediately to the National Trust. Sir Samuel Scott provided the money, but the Trust, with little expertise in estate management, asked her to continue to run the land until someone else could be found.

The National Trust was formed in January 1895 by Canon Rawnsley and Octavia Hill. Within ten years 24 properties were owned and in 1907 the National Trust Act was passed, giving the trust inalienable rights over the land. Canon Rawnsley, who had known Beatrix since she was 16 and was a great admirer of her paintings, had attempted to interest a publisher in *The*

Tarn Hows

Tale of Peter Rabbit by rewriting the story himself in verse. Fortunately they rejected the lines in which Peter rhymes with sweeter, and asked instead for prose.

Within a year *Peter Rabbit* had sold 50,000 copies and with the royalties Beatrix bought her first Lake District property, a field near Sawrey, then in 1905 she purchased Hill Top, a working farm. Later that year Norman Warne, her publisher, to whom to her parents' dismay she had become engaged, suddenly died. Hill Top was a refuge from grief and from her parents. An extension was built for the farmer and his family, leaving the seventeenth-century part for Beatrix whenever she was able to escape from London.

The following eight years saw 13 new books from Beatrix, and as her fame and royalties increased, she began to add to her properties. The solicitor she employed was William Heelis of Sawrey who, as she was absent for long periods, kept a watch over her interests.

There was consternation from her parents when in 1912 Mr Heelis asked her to marry him. By now Beatrix was 47 and a country solicitor was of course unsuitable, but despite the strain which made her ill, she was determined. At this point her brother came to the rescue, announcing to his parents that for the last seven years he had been secretly married himself!

Gradually Beatrix Potter, artist and storyteller, became Mrs Heelis, farmer and sheepbreeder. More farms and cottages were added to her estates, but although she was in sympathy with the aims of Canon Rawnsley and the National Trust, and contributed to their appeals, there were differences. Access was always a difficult matter. The Trust's first aim was to acquire and preserve open countryside to be enjoyed by the general public, a fact that today is sometimes overlooked by people who associate the Trust exclusively with stately homes. Beatrix, on the other hand, was more concerned with protecting the ancient farms and cottages. Farms needed managing efficiently if they were to survive, and visitors, she felt, should keep to footpaths.

But even for Mrs Heelis, the expert breeder of sheep, the fells were different. "It is always a pity to hear of visitors being turned back from fell land" she wrote on hearing that a farmer had closed a right of way. But then she never did mind a bit of mud.

ROUTE DESCRIPTION

Wharton Tarn

Leaving the visit to Tarn Hows for later in the walk, take the grassy path from the eastern end of the car park, which though staying close to the road, climbs through the bracken, short-cutting the bends, and continues through the trees. Coniston Water appears briefly, then descending through the wood to a ladder stile, a second stile to the right leads to Wharton Tarn. Set in an open field on the edge of the forest, it is an attractive spot, though the edges of the tarn are rather marshy, and covered with reeds and the aromatic

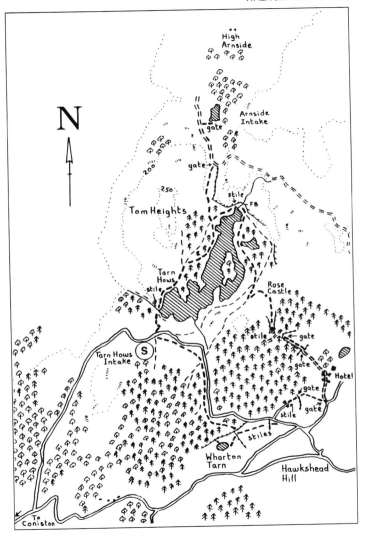

8.1

shrubby plants of bog myrtle.

Rose Castle Tarn

Climbing back over the stile, follow the waymarks through the fields towards Hawkshead Hill. On joining the lane turn left for a few yards, and then go right on the tarmac drive to Sawrey Ground. Sawrey means muddy place, but it seemed dry enough to us, and passing in front of the whitewashed cottage, you continue in the same direction through a gate. Crossing a small field to the edge of the wood, veer right across another field to where a gate leads onto the road.

Turn left up the driveway to the houses adjacent to the Yewfield Hotel, formerly the Tarn Hows Hotel, and going between the buildings the old road leads on up the hill. After a gate the path continues beside the wood before entering the trees at another gate. Crossing a forest road in the narrow neck of woodland, the right of way goes over a stile and back into the fields to pass to the right of Rose Castle. This isolated cottage, looking like something out of a Grimms fairy tale, may have connections with the Bishop of Carlisle, for his palace is also called Rose Castle.

Follow the drive out to join a track and turn right downhill towards Tarn Hows. Going straight across at the next junction, the path leads to a chalet in Rose Castle Plantation, which is used by the scouts. This small tarn, which is completely separate and a little higher than Tarn Hows, is retained by the small concrete dam, and a stream flows from it into the larger tarn.

High Arnside Tarn (*Arni's high hill pasture tarn*)

Continue beside Tarn Hows, surely the most photographed stretch of water in the Lakes, to reach the main path which loops round the northern end of the tarn. Originally made by combining several small swampy pools to provide water power for a saw mill, the tarn and its surroundings were landscaped in the 1850s by the Marshalls of Monk Coniston as an extension to their garden.

At the path junction on the far side of Tarn Hows, turn right, and go out to join the Mountain Road, an old unsurfaced road flanked by stone walls. Turning left on the road, which must once have been of some importance, soon the gate is reached to High Arnside Tarn. Like Tarn Hows it was created by James Marshall in the nineteenth century, and is named after the nearby farm which was given to the National Trust by Sir Samuel Scott in memory of his son who was killed in the war.

Tarn Hows (*Tarn hills*)

Retracing your steps to the path junction beside Tarn Hows, continue round the tarn on the main path through the trees. This path was constructed in 1993 with financial support from British Gas and the Countryside Commission

Rose Castle

to provide a walk right round the tarn, suitable for wheelchairs and pushchairs. Reaching the small dam across Tongue Gill, it is then only a short way back up the hill to the car park.

Though far busier than in Beatrix Potter's day, and on a sunny summer weekend with more cars than she would have believed possible, the tarn still manages to retain its charm. Artificial it may be, but for many this is their first and favourite tarn. And we owe it all to a little pig called Robinson.

WALK 8.2: HIGH WRAY AND BLELHAM TARN

Tarns:	Lily Pond
	Hodson's Tarn
	Normoss Tarn
	Blelham Tarn
Distance:	7 miles
Ascent:	750ft
Summary:	Easy walking through fields and forest to the shore of Windermere and a Gothic castle.
Starting Point:	(GR 353981) Hawkshead. Large car park which soon gets full.

"Damned scoundrel!" exclaimed Coleridge when, passing Blelham Tarn in November 1799, he caught sight of yet another of the houses of the wealthy that were annexing the edge of the lake at Ambleside. But though many more mansions were to be built on the eastern shore, the western side remained free from ostentatious display until the 1840s, when the Gothic extravagance of Wray Castle appeared.

Built by James Dawson, a Liverpool surgeon, Wray Castle has been variously execrated and admired. H.H. Symonds, founder of the Friends of the Lake District, thought it "grotesque", but surprisingly Wordsworth approved of the place, planted a mulberry tree in the grounds and commented that the castle "added a dignified feature to the interesting scenery in which it stands". Dr Dawson's wife was, however, far from impressed. It was her money, a family fortune founded on gin, that had been squandered. She refused to live in it and eventually her husband went bankrupt.

Close by the castle is the church of St Margaret's, which was also built by Dr Dawson, and here at the age of 27 the Rev Hardwick Drummond Rawnsley began his ministry. Born in 1851 and educated at Oxford University, Canon Rawnsley, as he later became, was granted the living by his cousin who was then the owner of Wray Castle. In the following year he married a local girl, Edith Fletcher, and the two of them were popular hosts to many celebrated guests.

It was at Wray that Rawnsley first met Beatrix Potter. The castle was rented as a holiday home by wealthy Victorians and in 1882 Beatrix, who was just 16 at the time, stayed here with her parents. The Potter family became friends with the young vicar whose enthusiasm for the landscape was to lead eventually to the formation of the National Trust.

While the grandiose mansions built by Manchester businessmen, many of them now hotels, restrict access to the eastern shores of Windermere, it is nature that presents the problems of approach to Blelham Tarn, for it is fringed with dense reed beds and a tangle of trees. The name Blelham Tarn is a tautology. The word 'tarn' is superfluous for Blelham means the Blue Pool, from *bla* which is Norse for blue, and *lumme*, an Old English word for a pool. The low-lying swampy land adjacent to the tarn, known as Blelham Bog, is a Site of Special Scientific Interest where the great-crested grebe nests on one of its few sites in the north of England.

It was late in the afternoon as we came back to Hawkshead and most of the visitors had left. A few disconsolate figures peered into the windows of the closed tourist office, or idly turned over the goods laid out in front of the gift shops. Hawkshead has a population of 600, but on a sunny summer weekend there will be many times that number milling about the huge car park and the souvenir shops that, like a moat and bailey, separate new from old in Hawkshead. The village, with its quaint little squares and whitewashed alleys is pleasant enough, but somehow it lacks a lived-in atmosphere and

Wray Castle

we were not sorry to turn our backs on the museum-like streets. After all, the pubs would be open soon and it was time for dinner.

ROUTE DESCRIPTION
Colthouse

From the large public car park at Hawkshead, go out to the bypass, built in 1974 to preserve the village, and turn left towards Ambleside. At the road bend a public footpath leads round to the right of Black Beck Cottage to a footbridge over Black Beck. Continuing over the fields to a kissing gate, and across another bridge to a second kissing gate, you fork right along the path signed to Colthouse.

Crossing Scar House Lane, it is a steep climb up the field to a stile into a rocky pasture, then waymarks point the way across two more stiles to reach a little lane at Croft's Head, where you turn right and the road is joined at Colthouse. Here Wordsworth lodged with Ann Tyson while he was at Hawkshead school. It was a happy household, and returning some years later from Cambridge University he expressed delight in seeing again "our rural dwelling".

Lily Pond and Hodson's Tarn

A few yards up the road to the left, by the gates of Gillbank, take the track which hairpins back towards Claife Heights. The bridleway goes above the house then climbs the hill with views of Hawkshead village and the Coniston Fells beyond. Reaching a gate through an unusual fence made of stone slabs set on end, the path continues through a scattering of larch and juniper, and after crossing a small stream carries on uphill through a gate in the deer fence.

Soon Lily Pond can be seen on the far side of the wall surrounded by rhododendrons. The water level is very low and you can just make out the dam at the far end, though we could see none of the water-lilies after which it was named. The view of the tarn improves as you continue to climb, and Hodson's Tarn, which was dammed in 1955 by the Freshwater Biological Association, can also be glimpsed through the trees a little further away. Beatrix Potter spent her summer holiday in 1882 exploring the little tarns on Claife Heights, and there are several more hidden in the trees, but there is no public access to them.

Normoss Tarn (*Northern bog tarn*)

The track climbs on through the forest, then at Junction 11 on the far side of a gate you briefly join the "White Post Route", a waymarked walk from the Windermere Ferry to Hawkshead. Keep straight on towards the ferry and Far Sawrey, and at the next forest road, Junction 10, the white posts are abandoned to continue straight across on the bridleway to Belle Grange. Descending through a young plantation, ahead in the distance you can see the Howgill Fells, the far range of hills with the scalloped edge.

Reaching a 5-way junction with a plethora of signposts, turn left along the forest road, but after 250 yards, leave the road and take the bridleway which runs just below it. From this rough track you can just make out the large shallow boggy tarn which lies below on the wooded Nor Moss, but though from the map this promises well, it looks better from a distance.

High Wray (*High secluded place*)

The route now becomes very indistinct for the track has been planted over and the path has been diverted to the left of the wall. Going through a gap, continue by the wall to reach a forest road where you turn right, still beside the wall, and down through the trees past Base Camp, a National Trust centre used to house volunteers on working holidays. Keep straight on down the unsurfaced track to leave the forest, and in the distance is Windermere with the Fairfield Horseshoe and Red Screes beyond.

Wray Castle

Reaching the road opposite High Wray Farm, turn right through the village

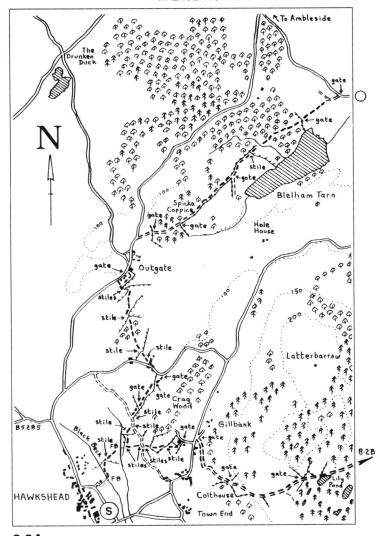

8.2A

of High Wray, which is still as quiet as the origins of its name suggest, and take the left fork at the road junction signed Wray Castle. The footpath to the lake leaves the road at the bend, and goes immediately over a stile into a field, then keeps beside the wall down to the shore of Windermere where there is a castellated boathouse.

Follow the byway to Wray church through a kissing gate and up the hill for a short way, then turn right over a stile into the Wray Castle Estate. This is all National Trust land and the footpath goes above the lake round the grassy hillside. The turrets and battlements of the mock castle soon come into view and on reaching the little rocky headland of Watbarrow Point, you climb up to a gate to join the metalled road which sweeps round the front of the building. There is a magnificent view of the head of Windermere, and even knowing that Beatrix Potter came from a wealthy family it is still a surprise to find they took over a castle as a holiday home.

When the castle was bought by the National Trust at a cost of £60,000, it was leased to the Youth Hostels Association, all, that is, except for three rooms in which Dr W.H. Pearsall founded the Freshwater Biological Association. It was a modest beginning, supported by private subscription with a small government grant, and Dr Pearsall continued with his usual mode of transport, a bicycle. Nowadays Wray Castle has a more prosaic use as a nautical electronics training school.

Blelham Tarn *(Dark blue pool)*

The tarmac drive leads past the Dower House down to St Margaret's church, where Canon Rawnsley was the minister, and the road is joined at a pair of impressive gates.

Turn right and past the entrance to Low Wray National Trust campsite, which has pitches for up to 200 tents, then turn left on the bridleway to Outgate. The track goes across the field to a kissing gate above the tarn and then winds on through what was once a wood, though most of the trees have now been felled. Blelham Tarn is fringed with dense reed beds, but there is a stile into the marshy woodland which is a Nature Reserve. Here Dr Pearsall carried out much valuable research into the history and ecology of the lakes and tarns.

Outgate *(Beyond the village)*

Crossing the stream, which comes from the now empty Blelham Fish Pond, the path goes through a stile by a gate and continues to the left of a wall. At the end of the tarn, keep straight on to Outgate on the gated track climbing by Spicka Coppice, and on to join the B5286. Turn left along the busy road through the hamlet of Outgate, where in 1783 Wordsworth waited with his brothers on his way home from school for the Christmas holidays. Within ten days his father was dead, and the memory of that expectant wait at the

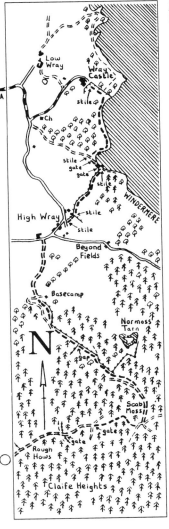

8.2B

junction of two roads was to have a profound effect on him.

Hawkshead (*Hawkr's small farmhouse*)

Immediately after the pub the footpath to Hawkshead goes behind the houses to a grassy walled enclosure, then continuing through a kissing gate crosses the field into a wood. Coming out into the open again, a ladder stile over a short bit of wall leads to another stile and Loanthwaite Lane.

Turning left past the farm, the path goes through a kissing gate on the right, then another kissing gate leads into the field below. Here we were joined by the muddy-pawed farm dog, who pranced joyfully round us as we followed the white marker posts by the hedge to a stile and down to join Scar House Lane.

Go left and then right through a small gate and across the fields to rejoin the outward route at the kissing gate, then retrace your steps back across the fields to Hawkshead, where the white-washed timber framed houses over-hanging narrow cobbled alleyways are little changed since the end of the eighteenth century.

WALK 8.3: CLAIFE HEIGHTS

Tarns:	Scale Ivy Tarn
	Brownstone Tarn
	High Moss Tarn
	Scale Head Tarn (Scale Tarn)
	Wise Een Tarn
	Moss Eccles Tarn
Distance:	5½ miles
Ascent:	1000ft
Summary:	A forest walk with a return by one of Beatrix Potter's favourite tarns.
Starting Point:	(GR 388955) Just west of Ferry House. Parking in the old quarry.
Alternative Start:	(GR 399959) Bowness. Large car park. The ferry runs every 20 minutes.

Among the larches and pines on the forest-covered low fells between Hawkshead and Windermere, the tarns of Claife Heights lie scattered as if left behind by the Ice Age. Yet though it was a glacier which carved the hollow of Windermere, and sent a separate tongue of ice looping westward to cut Blelham Tarn and Esthwaite Water, it did not form these tarns. Despite their lovely setting they are not natural, and nor is the forest, for this is a man-made landscape, planned and organised, but how well it has turned out!

Like most of Lakeland, these fells were natural woodland until Stone Age man, with flint axes fashioned from Langdale rock, began to make space for his crops. Although with the influx of Norse farmers more trees were felled, the area was still a deer park belonging to Furness Abbey in 1338. But during the seventeenth and eighteenth centuries it was industry that was to have the most dramatic impact on the fell, for in their desperate need for charcoal to fuel the smelt mills, men found coppicing too slow and eventually the woodland was stripped of its trees.

In 1794 John Christian Curwen decided to do something about it. Living on Belle Island, whose circular house was the first in England, he obtained an Act of Parliament to enclose Claife Heights and began to plant trees. The inclusion of larch was unpopular, but Mr Curwen was a practical man and he could see the commercial possibilities. And it is this forest that we see today, some owned by the National Trust, some by the Forestry Commission, and some still in private hands.

As we walked beneath the larches with the mist rising slowly like smoke from a charcoal burner's fire, and drifting softly among the tree-tops, the woods seemed enchanted. At any moment a ghostly figure might appear,

Windermere

and although the story is centuries old, there are still some who will not venture into the forest at night. Surely this is the only ghost whose exact position is recorded by the Ordnance Survey. The tale goes that one wild and stormy night in the fifteenth century the ferryman at the Nab heard a call from the distant shore and rowed across the lake. He returned alone, terrified and unable to speak, becoming so ill with a fever that he died a few days later. For many years after this no boatman would tend the ferry after dark, and the eerie cry of "Boat" was often heard during a storm. Finally the ghost was exorcised by a monk from Furness Abbey and the "Crier of Claife" was laid to rest in a quarry high in the woods.

It was then that we came upon the lost family. Seated quietly in the clearing they were waiting for help, and as we were looking at our map, obviously we must know what we were doing. Unfortunately the reason for our intense scrutiny was that we had just realised we too were lost. "Can you tell us where we are please?" they asked and on their faces was such an expectant look that we hadn't the heart to admit the truth. Instead we began feverishly to plot our location from our last known position. It seemed to take ages, and with every passing second we could see their confidence ebbing. Eventually we handed back their map with instructions on how to proceed. "Thank you" they said, "But we think we'll go back the way we came."

ROUTE DESCRIPTION

The Station (*The stopping place*)

The first part of the walk follows an official trail opened by the Duke of Edinburgh in 1966. Called rather unimaginatively 'The White Post Route', it starts in the disused quarry a short way along the Hawkshead road from the ferry. Ferry House, once a hotel, is now the headquarters of the Freshwater Biological Association, and we spent several fascinating hours on their open day learning about the myriad creatures that swim, float or just live under stones in the tarns.

From the quarry a track followed by a flight of steps leads to Thomas West's first station, one of a series of numbered viewpoints detailed in his 1778 Guide. The trees have long since obliterated the view, and only a crumbling ruin remains where Victorian tourists once came to the 'Pleasure-house' with its octagonal tower, whose coloured window-panes provided the choice of an autumn, winter or summer scene.

Scale Ivy Tarn (*Ivy hut tarn*)

Claife means steep hill, and going under an archway and through a little rocky cutting the path climbs a slope which certainly lives up to its name, leaving little breath to talk on the ascent through Station Scar Wood. The angle eases as Mitchell Knotts is reached, the hard work is now over and the path goes along the top of the wood, high above Windermere.

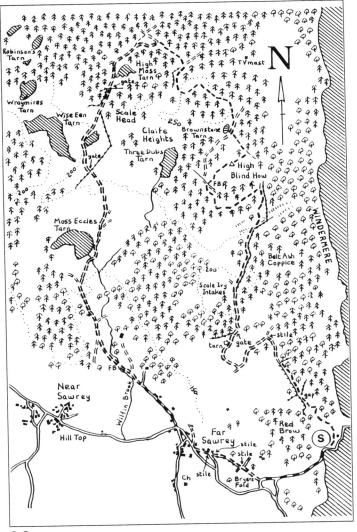

8.3

Becoming enclosed between stone walls, the path leads to White Post Junction 2, where you go left towards Far Sawrey along the bridleway. At Junction 3, turn uphill on the walled track, which is the footpath to Hawkshead, and the first of the Claife Heights tarns is met beside the path in the grassy pasture. Though nameless and little more than a pond, it deserves to be included as it contains more water than some of the named tarns passed on the walk.

Brownstone Tarn

The gated track leads into the woods then, after descending to a low point, you climb past some crags to White Post 4 where you turn left on the footpath to Hawkshead. Following more white posts, the path zigzags through the trees and two rocky clearings to a footbridge near the end of a forest road. Climbing now north-east to High Blind How (886ft), a path leads up to the stone trig point which marks the highest point on Claife Heights. These woods are roamed by Red deer who may be glimpsed moving almost silently through the trees. They do not herd, but keep in very small groups.

From the summit, and descending north-east, the path goes left to the forest road at White Post 5, by Brownstone Tarn. Now very overgrown, with dragonflies hovering and whirling to and fro across its shallow water, the tarn is only marked on the more recent OS maps.

High Moss Tarn (*High bog tarn*)

Turn right to Hawkshead, then fork left from the forest road at Junction 6, still on the footpath to Hawkshead, to continue past another rocky viewpoint from which the full length of the Troutbeck valley can be seen. Descending to Junction 7 at the end of a forest road, the footpath continues left through the trees to join a final forest road at the apex of a bend marked Junction 8.

This is as far as you go on the White Post Route. Turning left on the track, which is the bridleway to Sawrey, Belle Grange Beck is crossed, and as the forest road bends left, High Moss Tarn can be glimpsed among the trees. It is a disappointing boggy expanse, a small patch of open water which is diminishing under the encroaching growth of sedge and rush. At one time an observation hide stood on the far bank, for wildfowl are attracted to the water.

Scale Head Tarn and Wise Een Tarn (*Tarn above the hut, and Willow tarn*)

A gate leads out into the open and the bridleway descends gently past the stone dam of Scale Head Tarn. To the right is the vast expanse of Wise Een Tarn with its wooden boathouse on the far shore. Experts list a total of two dozen aquatic plants found here including yellow iris and white water-lily. All the tarns on Claife Heights have been examined in minute detail by the Freshwater Biologists from Ferry House, who have published complicated tables of their acidity and alkalinity and its variation over the years.

Moss Eccles Tarn

After a gate the track improves and the prettiest of all the tarns is reached. Surrounded by rhododendrons, with glacier smoothed and scratched rocks at the outflow bridged by a little dam, the tarn may have been the home of Mr Jeremy Fisher, for after Beatrix Potter married William Heelis in 1913 the couple lived at Castle Cottage, Far Sawrey and often rowed here in the evening. Beatrix sketched while her husband fished, and in 1926 she bought part of the tarn and stocked it with fish and water-lilies.

Far Sawrey (*Far muddy place*)

Carry on down the gated track to the fork. To the right is the bridleway to Near Sawrey and Beatrix Potter's house at Hill Top, which attracts even more visitors than Dove Cottage, but we go left to Far Sawrey. Near and Far Sawrey refer to the distance of the villages from Hawkshead which was once a very important centre of the woollen trade.

The bridleway fords the pretty little Wilfin Beck beside a footbridge and then the tarmac road from Righting House is joined. This leads past the Old Vicarage to Far Sawrey and the Sawrey Hotel, where the bar is named the Claife Crier after the ghostly legend.

The Ferry

Forking left opposite the village hall on the footpath to the ferry, follow the track uphill. Over to the right you can see St Peter's church which was built in 1869. Keep by the wall past the houses and the Riding Centre to a kissing gate, then go down the field with Windermere ahead. After another kissing gate, you cross a lane and go straight on down a shady track overhung with laurels to reach the road to the ferry.

Beatrix Potter was a frequent ferry passenger after her mother moved to Lindeth How, and there has been a ferry on Windermere for at least a thousand years for this was the route that linked Hawkshead to Kendal. In 1635 there was a major disaster when all 47 members of a wedding party were drowned. It was a very busy packhorse route, and the horses with their heavy loads were rowed across the strait. Though still busy at peak season with car traffic queuing in rows, the ferry is a delightful way to travel, with the feeling that at last the holiday has begun.

Larch cones

179

9: Grizedale Forest Tarns

WALK 9.1: GRIZEDALE FOREST

Tarns:	Grizedale Tarn
	Grizedale Tarn Small
	Juniper Tarn
	Gooseyfoot Tarn
	High Man Tarn
Distance:	8 miles
Ascent:	700ft
Summary:	Easy walking on forest tracks with splendid views of the high fells.
Starting Point:	(GR 336944) Grizedale Forest Visitor Centre, 3 miles south of Hawkshead. Car park.
Alternative Start:	(GR 343965) Moor Top car park and picnic area.

Glancing at the map of Grizedale Forest, with its serried ranks of mathematically arranged bottle-brush shapes, one might expect merely another commercial plantation with only one consideration: growing timber as a crop, and doing it as quickly and as economically as possible. But though anyone who has visited the valley will know that Grizedale is not like that, even those who are familiar with the forest may be surprised by the sheer variety of trees to be found.

For a start Grizedale is not all conifers, and much of the valley is covered in broad-leaved trees. As well as beech, a southern import, and sycamore, introduced to this country in about 1550, there are the traditional native hardwoods, oak, hazel, alder, wych-elm and birch. In the spring the wild cherry, rowan and bird cherry are a mass of blossom, while hidden on stream banks may be found the rare small-leaved lime. Even among the conifers there is little uniformity, for each species is suited to its habitat, the windswept heights having distinctly different trees from the sheltered valley sides.

The oak of the Grizedale woods is the sessile oak. Sessile means stalkless and it is the acorns that distinguish this tree, which thrives on the acid Lake District soil, from the pedunculate or long-stalked oak. Once the oaks were coppiced to provide timber for charcoal, which fed the voracious appetites of the smelting furnaces, and bark, the source of tannin for curing leather. But now the trees have been allowed to grow tall, with only the surrounding stumps a clue to the past.

For most people conifers are less easy to recognise than oak, ash and

180

Juniper Tarn

sycamore, which at least in summer have obvious differences, but even among the conifers each has its own distinctive characteristics. All are introduced species save one. Scots pine is a native and being tolerant of its growing conditions is found both in lowland communities and on the tops. It is easiest to recognise when mature, for then the upper trunk and boughs turn a distinctive orange red.

Scots pine, and also the Lodgepole pine and the Corsican pine, may be distinguished by their needles which are grouped in pairs, while firs, such as the Douglas fir, have softer needles which grow singly, but the most widespread evergreen is undoubtedly spruce. Spruce has needles growing separately on little woody pegs and the tree, which is tolerant of the worst conditions, is tough, and is even reputed to be resistant to sheep, a quality few others can match. There are two common species, and while the needles of the Norway spruce, the Christmas tree, snag and scratch as you push your way through them, Sitka spruce, which is more blue in colour, is the 'bovver boy' of the woods, a tough adversary indeed for anyone forced to grapple with its savagely sharp spines.

The larch is not an evergreen, and each autumn as its branches turn colour the woods are splashed with yellow and gold. The needles grow in tufts and in the spring the female flowers are like little red shaving brushes. There are two basic forms, the European and the Japanese, but the variety most usually planted nowadays is a hybrid of the two.

Managed it may be, carefully planted, cropped and replanted, but Grizedale Forest is perhaps closer to Lakeland as it used to be, for once the open fellsides were covered in trees, with only the highest summits projecting above the continuous canopy of green, and then a squirrel might travel from Low Furness to Langdale without ever touching the ground.

ROUTE DESCRIPTION

Grizedale Tarn (*Pig's valley tarn*)

On the opposite side of the road from the Visitor Centre, originally the outbuildings of the short-lived Grizedale Hall which was built in 1903 and demolished in 1956, a rough track climbs the hillside. After 200 yards a footpath turns off over a step stile in the wall beside a gate, then crossing the fields to a wooden stile, re-enters the forest. It is nearly sixty years since the Forestry Commission started planting here, but the older woodland was established by the Ainslies, former owners of Grizedale Hall. This is a working forest, and with a continuous cycle of felling and replanting it is forever changing.

Descending to ford a beck, the path then climbs on, straight across a forest road and up a little rocky staircase, and as it continues to climb, the view opens out across the forest to encompass the Coniston Fells. Reaching another forest road, turn left to the crossroads, and Grizedale Tarn lies just

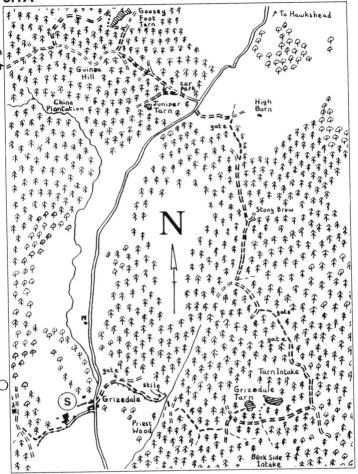

ahead. The only natural tarn in the forest, it sits beside a rocky knoll in a glacier scoured hollow with a platform jutting out over the clear water. Here in April spotted frogs crawl along the muddy bottom, and as we stood watching them, a group of children shouted with excitement "There's one, there's another one, and another; there's ever such a lot!".

Grizedale Tarn Small

Return to the track junction and turn left along the forest road for 200 yards to where a little path, marked by a wooden post with the letter S, leads through the trees to a second tarn. The S denotes a sculpture, and by the water is one of about 50 such creations in the forest. Both tarns share the same name and though this second tarn is also known as Grizedale Tarn Small, it is in fact now the larger of the two.

Moor Top

Continue along the forest road, then turning left at the T-junction the road soon deteriorates to a muddy track. Reaching a high fenced enclosure, erected to keep the deer away from the young trees, go through the gate, which has an ingenious latch for horse riders. The fells of the Fairfield Horseshoe now come into view, and the V-shape on the skyline marks the Kirkstone Pass with Caudale Moor and the Eastern Fells beyond.

The grassy path leaves the enclosure at another gate, then joins a forest road where you turn right. Reaching a T-junction in about 300 yards, turn right, then immediately fork left downhill to join a major forest road at the apex of a bend.

Keeping left the surroundings are now more open, with good views of Ambleside beneath the rounded bulk of Red Screes. In 300 yards, at the next bend under a power line, the track is abandoned and you follow a path down to leave the forest at a tall narrow gate. Joining a track, this leads left past some scattered juniper bushes and out to the road at the high point of Moor Top.

Juniper Tarn

Go through the car park and picnic area, then fork left on the forest road to reach Juniper Tarn. Surrounded by rhododendrons and tall conifers, yellow irises fringe the water which is retained by a low earth dam. The shipping magnate Harold Brocklebank, who bought Grizedale Hall from the Ainslies in 1903, created this tarn for his small son's miniature steamboat, but only one or two of the junipers remain for they do not like shady conditions.

Gooseyfoot Tarn

Retracing your steps, turn left uphill along the adjacent forest road and keep straight on at the crossroads. When the top of the hill is reached turn right, and in a few yards a track leads to the concrete dam of Gooseyfoot Tarn. This long narrow tarn, said to resemble the web foot of a waterfowl, has another dam at the far end and was originally an emergency water supply for Hawkshead. In the early 1960s the Forestry Commission worked in conjunction with the Wildfowler's Association to re-establish a colony of greylag geese here.

9.1B

High Man Tarn (*High cairn tarn*)

Heading due north, make your way out through the trees on the far side of the tarn to join another forest road where you turn left. The road curves round, and in ¼ mile you come to a T-junction. Turn right and keep on the main track, ignoring the first turn to the right and the second two turns to the left, and climb to the top of the hill by the power lines.

Now go left along the track which heads south past a wireless mast and a second much higher mast which replaces a former fire tower. At nearly a thousand feet this is the highest point of the walk. A few steps down the track to the left gives a view of High Man Tarn. This pretty tarn in a grassy clearing has been omitted from the Forestry Commission's own map to discourage visitors. Though it was probably constructed for the shooting, it is now an ecologically sensitive area which is managed principally for the conservation of wildlife, so please don't go any closer.

Grizedale (*Pig's valley*)

The footpath continues along the broad boggy ridge of Grizedale Moor with fine views of Coniston Old Man to the north-west, easily identified by the little bump of its cairn on the top. The path swings round to head south-west, and then a forest road is reached. Turning left, go straight across the next staggered junction, and fork left down through Park Plantation. Planting began on these slopes in 1952 with Sitka spruce above and Douglas fir and Japanese larch below.

Joining a forest road, turn right for a few yards, then go left again down a footpath, where in spring the bracken slopes are covered in daffodils, and going past a farm, the Grizedale Centre is at the end of the road. As well as a shop and cafe there is a most interesting Visitor Centre, which depicts the history of Grizedale and is well worth a visit. There is also the little Theatre in the Forest, which has regular performances by both musicians and entertainers, as well as illustrated lectures on the Lake District.

WALK 9.2: SATTERTHWAITE TO ARNSBARROW TARN

Tarns:	Arnsbarrow Tarn
	Wood Moss Tarn (Hob Gill Tarn)
Distance:	4¹/₂ miles
Ascent:	800ft
Summary:	The pathless moor, which can be confusing in mist, adds adventure to an easy forest walk.
Starting Point:	(GR 337919) Satterthwaite. Small car park ¹/₄ mile south of the village.

In the warmth of the spring sunshine the trees were just beginning to unfurl their leaves, the white-washed houses shone, and beside the road daffodils gleamed bright gold. Outside the Eagle's Head a couple of cycles leaned against the wall, but there were few people about for it was still early in the season and Satterthwaite dozed quietly in the sun.

Satterthwaite is an attractive small village with a pub, the parish church of All Saints, a school and a post office. As its name, summer pasture, suggests, the village had its origins in Viking times when Norsemen sailed into Rusland Pool in their long ship and built a farm at Rusland. During the summer they took their pigs to Grizedale and the sheep up to their farm at Satterthwaite. By the Middle Ages all the valley belonged to Furness Abbey and the woodland became a valuable source of coppiced timber for the charcoal burners who supplied the iron ore bloomeries. Now belonging to Grizedale Forest Park, the woodlands fit naturally into the landscape.

Leaving the valley we began to climb away from the village into the trees, and as we came out into an open felled area high on the moor, we could see the snow-capped peaks of the Coniston Fells, the Old Man and Wetherlam looking temptingly close, but ahead the track, churned by tractors and forest machinery, was a sea of mud.

It was then that we heard a subdued mutter of engines and a few minutes later three brightly coloured motorbikes bounced and slithered their way up the track towards us, but as the leading bike reached the morass, its front wheel sank to the hub and they stopped. Propping his bike on its stand, one of the following riders waded into the mud and began to pull at the submerged wheel.

"Do you mind" we asked, "if we take some photos?" "Well, all right, but it's not for a magazine is it?" they responded doubtfully. "We get a lot of people saying we've no right to be here, yet this track's classified as a road."

Motorcyclists have had a bad press from many walkers, but those we have met have been responsible, friendly people, and as we talked they explained that they were always very careful to check which paths were open to them. Then with mud spraying from their wheels they were away, waving a cheery good-bye, and in a few minutes the sound of their engines was gone.

As we emerged onto the open moor the winter-whitened stalks of purple moor-grass gleamed in the sunshine above the black expanse of heather, while in the wetter places was the occasional, almost luminous patch of bright, yellow-green sphagnum moss. In the distance were a couple of walkers, but these were the last figures to be seen all day.

Arnsbarrow Tarn is elusive. Hiding shyly in a hollow it can easily be missed in bad weather but, with its almost circular shape reflecting a clear blue sky, it was at its best. Returning to the forest edge we came down to Bell Beck and back into the trees where wide tracks, with the fresh, sharp smell of newly cut logs piled in great heaps, led us to Wood Moss Tarn.

"Wood Moss Tarn is a Wildlife Sanctuary Area and we are trying to maintain its peace and quiet" said the forester. The tarn's inhabitants thought otherwise. Screeching and squawking as they circled above the tarn, hundreds of black-headed gulls were landing, taking off, and quarrelling with each other. Like a busy airport there was a cacophony of sound. They were making far more noise than half a dozen motorbikes.

ROUTE DESCRIPTION

Grizedale Forest (*Pig's valley forest*)

Moor Lane leads from the little car park along the edge of the forest, where we found our first primroses of the year, and past a seat with a beautiful view of Satterthwaite, whose white-washed cottages cluster round the square towered little church, rebuilt in 1840 by Mr Ainslie of Grizedale Hall. But it is too soon to stop, and after a gate the track dips to ford a little stream. Crossing straight over the forest road beyond, the track climbs the hill at an easy angle through the trees, and crosses another forest road, then as the brow of the hill is reached the Coniston Fells appear ahead above the trees. Though the track is still classified as a road, the boggy section at the top, which is easily skirted on foot, is a major obstacle to motorcyclists. This was the route that led from Force Forge, the site of a medieval bloomery, to Parkamoor, an ancient sheep farm belonging to the monks of Furness Abbey. Parkamoor was given to the National Trust in 1968.

Arnsbarrow Tarn (*The tarn by Arne's burial mound*)

A final forest road is crossed, and the old track continues to the edge of the trees. Go through the gate and turn left to follow the fence uphill. It is easy walking on the edge of the open moor with a bit of a path to follow through the heather and bracken.

187

When the forest boundary turns away, continue in the same direction to the heathery knoll of Heel Toe Hill. There is a very extensive view from the top, with the whole of the Coniston Fells on show. To the north-east lie the Helvellyn Range, the Eastern Fells and the Howgill Fells, and you can even see as far as the Yorkshire hills and flat-topped Ingleborough. To the south is Morecambe Bay and the windmills on Kirkby Moor, while south-west is the dark shape of Black Combe.

Heading south-west down a boggy little valley, Arnsbarrow Tarn is reached, ¼ mile from the fence corner. Hidden round the corner in a large boggy depression on the hummocky moor, the tarn contains white water-lilies and the clear water is fringed with sweet-smelling bog myrtle.

Bethecar Moor

Return to the forest boundary, heading south-east along the adjacent valley, and then go east round the lower slopes of Arnsbarrow Hill. Bold green dots march across the contours of the Ordnance Survey map, but on the ground there is no sign of the path. Our first visit to this area was in an orienteering event and Bethecar Moor is a real test of navigation, especially in mist, but the forest edge is an infallible guide making it impossible to remain lost, at least not for very long.

Skirting round the man-eating bog at the head of Yew Beck, continue near the fence, past little waterfalls overhung by holly bushes and clumps of juniper, and soon you reach a broken wall. Keep well over to the right and follow the ravine down to the bottom, where Bell Beck is crossed to a step stile into the forest.

Wood Moss Tarn

The little path runs along the edge of an area newly felled in 1994, but as the forest landscape is continually changing it will soon be green again with young trees. Joining the end of a forest track, this leads to a forest road where you go left and then immediately right on a grassy footpath through the trees.

This wooded hillside was the route by which Franz von Werra escaped from Grizedale Hall when it was a prisoner-of-war camp. He was recaptured on the slopes of Hesk Fell after five days, but later made a successful escape from Canada.

Meeting another forest road detour left for a few yards to view Wood Moss Tarn, which was constructed in the 1960s with the intention of reintroducing beavers to the area. Though the project was never carried through, the tarn is maintained as a quiet and undisturbed sanctuary to conserve the wildlife, so please don't go any closer. On the far bank you can see wooden observation hides and it is possible to obtain permission from the Forestry Commission to use these. The long shallow tarn has a large colony of black-headed gulls nesting on a grassy island, but many other bird species are also attracted to the area.

Satterthwaite[9.2B]
(*Summer dwelling*)

Returning to the right of way, this crosses straight over the forest road to enter the plantation by an unusual trap door stile. The raucous cries of the gulls can still be heard and there are glimpses of the tarn through the trees.

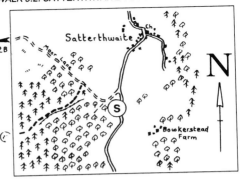

9.2A

Leaving through another trap door, continue along the hillside to join a track where you turn left. In 50 yards the forest road that leads into the Wildlife Sanctuary is crossed, then the track continues through a newly felled area and it is about ⅓ mile back to join Moor Lane.

9.2B

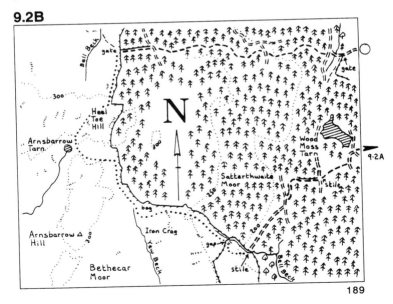

10: Southern Tarns

WALK 10.1: HIGH DAM

Tarns:	Low Dam
	High Dam
Distance:	2 miles
Ascent:	400ft
Summary:	The shortest walk in the book, perfect for a warm afternoon.
Starting Point:	(GR 369883) Finsthwaite. High Dam car park.

The little shop at the entrance to Stott Park Bobbin Mill was bright and welcoming and we were just in time to make up the numbers for a guided tour. Inside the mill the workshop floor was deep in wood shavings, the ancient machinery glistened with new oil, and above our heads the shafts, belts and wheels clattered busily.

Leaning against a saw bench the guide, a volunteer from English Heritage, showed us the baskets of bobbin blanks and a desperately dangerous looking piece of machinery which drilled the holes, then a retired bobbin-maker demonstrated how the bobbins were finished on a lathe. Unlike any wood turning we had seen before, this was a sudden and dramatic process. As the sharp steel knife touched the spinning cylinder of birch, there was a sudden shriek of cutting timber, and a curving ribbon of wood flew into the air. Another touch of a different cutter, and the bobbin was complete.

The Victorian machinery in the mill is kept in working order and having seen the wood being roughed out into blocks and the various stages involved in shaping, boring and drying, we were then ushered upstairs. The groups are kept small on account of the fragile upper floors, with dire warnings about where not to tread, and we tiptoed round the drums where the finished bobbins were polished with paraffin wax. Downstairs again there was a steam engine to admire, a working water turbine, and we visited the drying room and the coppice barn.

Stott Park Mill was built in 1835 by John Harrison, originally to provide bobbins and reels for the Lancashire cotton trade, though later the business expanded to make dozens of different sorts of bobbins, as well as a wide range of wooden handles. In its heyday up to 25 men and boys were employed, but the hours were long, the machinery dangerous and the large quantity of dust produced, a health hazard. The mill was powered by water from the nearby millpond whose water came from High Dam, up on the fellside. In time the wheel was superseded by a turbine and then a small

Stott Park Bobbin Mill

steam engine was installed. When it finally closed in 1971, due to Scandinavian competition and the decline of the cotton industry, Stott Park was one of the last working bobbin mills in the Lake District.

As such huge quantities of wood were needed, the mills were built near the raw material. There were many similar mills in the surrounding district, and the local woodland had been previously coppiced for charcoal burning, swill and hoop-making. Coppicing goes back for centuries and although such woodland contains few, if any, mature trees, it does not destroy the woods.

191

The natural life of a birch tree is little longer than a man's, but when the stools are repeatedly cut down and allowed to grow again, they will survive for hundreds of years. Oak, ash and sycamore were also used, though the bobbins were usually made of birch, and the open heather-clad hillside behind the mill was planted in the 1850s with both oak and birch to provide more timber for Stott Park Mill.

Our first sight of High Dam was when orienteering on Finsthwaite Heights, but as we ran past the tarn there was no time to admire the scenery, for in orienteering every second counts. Over the years we competed several more times on these hills, and always in too much of a hurry to stop. More time was needed, and as we emerged from the mill into the afternoon sunshine, we turned up the hillside for that long awaited visit to High Dam, surely one of the prettiest tarns in Lakeland.

ROUTE DESCRIPTION

Low Dam

The track leads uphill from the car park to a gate, then taking the left fork you climb beside the stream to reach the pretty little tarn of Low Dam, which is surrounded by larch and silver birch. At the foot of the dam a rusty old valve pipe is a reminder of the tarn's purpose when the reservoir was constructed to provide Stott Park Mill with constant water pressure for a turbine, which in 1858 replaced the original waterwheel.

High Dam

Crossing the stream, the path climbs to the higher stone dam where a little stream flows over the slipway and down to Low Dam. This must surely be one of the loveliest tarns in the Lake District. It was made in 1835 when the original Finsthwaite Tarn was enlarged to power a 32ft diameter waterwheel at Low Stott Park. Even though it is artificial, the 10 acre stretch of water, with little rocky headlands, and surrounded by larch trees and Scots pine, reminds one of a Scottish loch. The fishing is free and according to the *Angler's Guide* it "has the distinction of being one of the few Lakeland tarns with a thriving population of Rudd".

After crossing the dam, follow the neatly constructed path that encircles the tarn. Little bridges span boggy areas, and beyond the two small islands and a footbridge the right of way to Rusland goes off to the left. Staying by High Dam, the path climbs along the slopes of Great Green How, which remains open moorland, and in spring is scattered with clumps of primroses, then rounding the end of the tarn the path goes through a gap in the wall.

A kissing gate leads temptingly through the wall on the left, but the circular path, which continues round the tarn, is at the time of writing the only official way to return to the car park. However there are plans to open a concession path which will be signposted when it has been agreed.

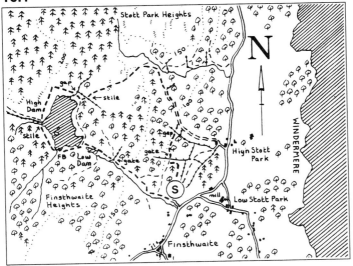

Proposed Route of Concession Path

Turning left through the kissing gate the path descends the bracken covered hillside towards Stott Park Heights. Wending its way through rocky knolls and boulders with a sprinkling of trees, the path then bends right and down to the stream at a concrete plinth.

Don't cross the stream, but fork right on an indistinct path, which soon becomes very obvious for it goes along the remains of an old wall. The path then becomes enclosed to form a track and passing a group of ancient yews, continues down through the woodland as a narrow walled lane.

After about 250 yards, the concession path leaves the lane to turn right through a gap in the wall. The path goes through a small gate in the fence and the car park is just beyond.

WALK 10.2: HAY BRIDGE

Tarns:	Black Beck Tarn
	White Moss Tarn
Distance:	3 miles
Ascent:	250ft
Summary:	A gentle walk for the naturalist through a wide variety of

different habitats. Occasionally the fenland can become impassable due to flooding.

NOTE Dogs must be on a lead in the Nature Reserves.

Starting Point: (GR 329874) Unfenced road 1¹/₂ miles north of Bouth. Parking on the verge near Low Longmire Farm.

PRIVATE said the forbidding notice. We consulted the map, surely it was a right of way? The lane led through the entrance to the Hay Bridge Nature Reserve, and temptingly on into the trees. "Can I help?" enquired the young man as his car drew up beside us. He was, he said, a musician staying at Low Hay Bridge. "Do call at the house" he urged, "we're having a recruiting drive."

We had only gone a short way down the lane when we came to a delightful small tarn, unmarked on the map, but buzzing with life. It is known as Black Beck Tarn from the sluggish meandering beck that rises here. A wooden platform juts out above the water, where white water-lilies and bogbean flower surrounded by a fringe of bulrushes and yellow iris. A little further on is White Moss Tarn, but while this does appear on the map it has obviously been extended since the surveyors passed this way.

Arriving at Low Hay Bridge, where a stone-built Lakeland barn houses the museum, we were enthusiastically welcomed by Anne Frahm, the daughter of Mrs Tissie Fooks, founder of the 220 acre reserve. "I'm sorry it's still so disorganised" she said, ushering us into the museum where stags' heads mingled with leopard skins and African memorabilia. With plans to modernise and update the exhibits and develop the library, they had, she said, a lot of work to do.

Anne told us how her mother had established the reserve in 1971 as a memorial to her husband, and created the museum to house his collection. Major Herbert Fooks spent his life working with wild animals, much of it in Africa and India. He was keeper of the Queen's wildfowl in London, and came to Grizedale in the 1950s, where he set up an educational centre to teach deer management to the foresters. The Deer Museum is a continuation of this work and the main aim of the society is to involve young people in the study and understanding of wildlife in the environment.

The president of the Hay Bridge Nature Reserve Society is Walter Lloyd, perhaps the best known charcoal burner in the country after his TV appearance, and in the woodland behind the museum is a reproduction of a coppice workers' settlement, with a bark-peeler's hut, a half-section of a charcoal pitstead, and also a restored potash pit. The main glory of Hay Bridge, however, is the deer, for the Rusland Red deer herd is one of the finest in the country.

We were so impressed with their work that we joined the society and were given a map and a number of interesting information sheets which told us about the plants, birds and animals to be found on the reserve, the history of the Rusland valley and the identification of deer. As a member you receive regular newsletters about activities at the centre, nature notes, and an events calendar. However this walk around the reserve follows rights of way which are open to everyone.

ROUTE DESCRIPTION

Black Beck Tarn

Just past Low Longmire Farm a footpath leads into the fields near a little barn and continues by the wall to a step stile. Rounding a knoll, the path does not go where it is marked on the OS map, but stays in the same field to follow the wall along past the gorse bushes to a step stile in the corner. "When the gorse is out of flower, then kissing's out of fashion" goes the old saying, but the almost continuous display is because there are two sorts of gorse the European variety flowers early in the spring and the Western later in the year.

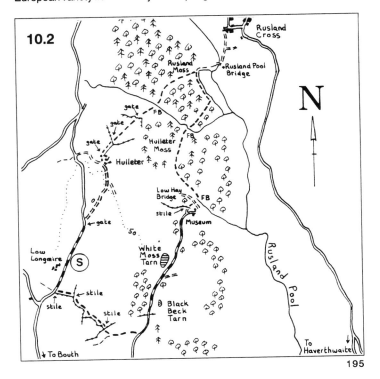

Heading straight on across the fell, a tarmac lane is joined where you turn left to a cattle grid and the gate into Hay Bridge Nature Reserve. This private reserve was created in 1971 as a deer sanctuary to provide both Red and Roe deer with a quiet area.

Almost immediately the footpath passes Black Beck Tarn, which was established in 1973 by flooding a low-lying area to create an open water habitat. The tarn with its small island is frequented by mallard, coot, moorhen, little grebe and reed bunting.

White Moss Tarn

The right of way continues along the tarmac lane which follows a natural depression through the reserve, with Hulleter Scar woods to the west and bracken covered slopes to the east. Keep straight on at the fork, following the signs to the museum, and to the left is White Moss Tarn. Toads live in the stones of the dam and there is an official 'Toad Crossing' linking Black Beck Tarn with White Moss Tarn. The tarn, which lies in a glacial hollow, was excavated at the same time as Black Beck Tarn, but it is not really new as pollen analysis showed there was a lake here until about 8000 years ago. The habitat is more open and the tarn is set on the edge of the fields, but the little wooded island encourages many nesting birds and it is also visited by rare greylag geese and goosanders.

Hay Bridge Museum

The grassy verges on either side of the tarmac track are full of wild flowers and a great variety of grasses. Don't follow the track down to the museum, but fork left on the footpath to Hulleter and Rusland. The Hay Bridge Deer Museum is essentially a private teaching museum and has displays of four

species of deer as well as a naturalist's collection of specimens. Turn right through a gap in the wall and go down through the bluebell wood to a ladder stile and across the track to a footbridge.

Hay Bridge and Rusland Mosses
(*High bridge and Rolf's land bogs*)
Entering the trees of the Wildlife Sanctuary the footpath, marked with white posts, goes along the waterlogged edge of the peaty raised bog of Hay Bridge Moss. In the drier parts, silver birch and pine have

The modern charcoal burner

become established, and scattered among the trees are many clumps of the rare royal fern. This was once much more common until the Victorians found it was a good medium for growing orchids and dug most of it up.

The path bends right through sweet-smelling bog myrtle, heather and hare's tail cotton-grass, and in the distance lie the wooded slopes of Rusland Heights. Two small footbridges are then crossed, and the path emerges from the trees into fenland which floods in the very high tides of spring and autumn. Rusland Pool is slow-flowing and the word 'pool' is old English for a series of wet, marshy areas, though the river is now dredged regularly. On the far side of the valley, beside the road, are the famous Rusland Beeches, which since 1953 have been protected by a tree preservation order.

The path follows the edge of a ditch, where among the reeds and rushes is a wide variety of plants including ragged robin and the fleshy leaves of orpine, while in the water are the pretty white flowers of water crowfoot. As the obvious path bends away to Rusland Pool Bridge, turn sharply left on a narrow trod to enter the trees of Rusland Moss, a National Nature Reserve where if you are lucky you may see both Roe and Red deer. Here we found the purple marsh lousewort and that rare cousin of the buttercup, the globe flower with its incurved golden petals.

Hulleter

Leaving the reserve over a couple of footbridges, the right of way crosses the fields to a gateway, then aiming to the right of the buildings, climbs to Hulleter Farm. Go through the yard, then turn left along the farm drive. Forking right in 100 yards, the track climbs gently and looking back you can see Rusland church standing on a little green hill in the middle of the trees. Arthur Ransome, who thought Rusland churchyard one of the most peaceful places on earth, was buried there in 1967. The track climbs past a fenced muddy pool, built to water the cattle, and the unfenced road is joined at a gate where you turn left back towards Low Longmire Farm.

WALK 10.3: BIGLAND TARN AND CANNY HILL

Tarns:	Bigland Tarn
	Back Reddings Allotment Tarn (Bigland Trout Fishery)
	Canny Hill Tarn
Distance:	5 miles
Ascent:	900ft
Summary:	Easy walking through woodland and rough pastures.
Starting Point:	(GR 345834) Layby on B5278 1 mile south of Haverthwaite.
Alternative Start:	(GR 350843) Haverthwaite Station (adds an extra mile).

There was no doubt about it, we were lost. Well, not exactly lost, but although we knew we were on Bigland Allotment the ground didn't fit the map, or was it the other way about? On a grey dismal day, amid an expanse of rough, tussocky moor, we stopped and thought again. The trouble with this fell is the paths. Those marked on the map have vanished, while in their place a maze of new ones has appeared. This was supposed to be an easy walk; one for an off day, a leisurely look at the tarns above Haverthwaite, and a return in time for tea. But unless we got ourselves sorted pretty soon, it was going to be a very long day.

We could have driven to Haverthwaite. It was only half an hour in the car, but we had decided to approach Bigland Tarn in style. We were going by boat. By boat and by train in fact, for there was no hurry and the journey would be part of the fun.

More than a century ago this was the new way to the Lakes. An extension of the Furness Railway had been laid to the foot of Windermere, a restaurant had been built, an orchestra hired for the summer, and not only had a long platform been constructed for the trains, there was an extensive jetty too, with room for no less than three steamers. Barrow folk, newly wealthy from expanding trade, and people from the Lancashire towns, would arrive on the train, embark on the steamer for a cruise to Ambleside, and then in late afternoon they would return. We liked the idea of travelling in style, but as we were staying near Ambleside our journey would have to be in the opposite direction.

The railway had reached Lakeside at the foot of Windermere in 1869, but there were steamers on Windermere even earlier, for the first paddle boats were griming their way up the lake in 1845. There are three cruisers now, *Teal*, *Tern* and *Swan*, but though *Tern* was once driven by steam, now she, like her companions, is diesel.

Down the lake we glided, past the battlements of Wray Castle, past the wooded slopes of Claife Heights, the little island of Lady Holme and the tiny Hen Holme, then after a brief stop at Bowness, we swept past Belle Island and on to Lakeside where our train awaited. Railway enthusiasts swarmed over the platform, and clouds of steam drifted up from the engine as we climbed aboard. Then with a creak and a groan of ancient ironwork, slowly the train moved out of the station.

Some hours later in the mist high on the fellside, our approach in style still seemed an excellent way, and we were looking forward to the return trip. But already it was late in the afternoon and the train would not wait. Then as the wall loomed out of the mist we knew where we were. There was just enough time. We hurried down through Low Wood, back across the river, and panted up the hill to Haverthwaite and the station. At least the train knew the way back.

Lakeside and Haverthwaite Railway

ROUTE DESCRIPTION

From Haverthwaite Station

If you are arriving by train, cross the busy A590, the most dangerous part of the walk, and follow the road through Haverthwaite past the Anglers Arms. At the timber yard, which makes children's playground equipment, take the footpath through the yard and across the field beside the river to Low Wood Bridge, then keep straight on up the hill to the start of the walk.

Bigland Tarn

Almost opposite the layby on the B5278 the footpath, signed to Grassgarth Heights, leads through a thicket of the invasive Japanese knotweed into Birk Dault Wood. Climbing through the trees past clumps of rhododendrons and tall fronds of royal fern an open area is reached. A track is crossed, and the path climbs on through a larch plantation and then through mixed broad-leaved woodland to a little gate. The path continues above the stream and past an old barn, and to the left is Bigland Hall which dates from 1125. This large country house was the home of the Bigland family for more than 850 years, but in 1991 financial circumstances forced George Bigland to sell the estate and part of the house is now used as holiday flats.

Arriving at Bigland Tarn, go through the kissing gate to the left and along the shore, past a small boathouse and a little jetty. The 13 acre tarn is a coarse fishery controlled by Bigland Hall Estate and is open all year, with roach, rudd, carp, tench, pike and perch lurking beneath the lily pads. According to the experts, the rare waterweed *Elodea nuttallii* (no relation) can be found here.

On the far side of this natural tarn is the aptly named Grassgarth Heights, which reaches 673ft, while the slopes rising to Bigland Heights are covered in bracken. In 1799 a beggar was found collapsed here in the snow. Rescued and taken back to Cartmel, he insisted on remaining in his wet clothes, caught a fever and died. In his clothes were found a false kidney stone, a forged medical certificate, and 185 guineas. The money was used to buy four fields near Grange and the annual rent from this was divided among the poor.

Fisherman at Bigland Tarn

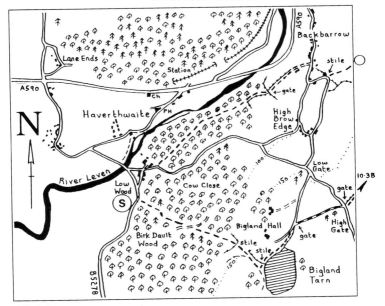

10.3A

Back Reddings Allotment Tarn

The footpath becomes a track, then joining the tarmac road from the hall, you fork right over the cattle grid, signposted to the trout fishery, clay pigeon ground and archery, some of the estate's country sports activities. Follow the tarmac track through the rhododendrons, then at High Gate cross the road and take the footpath to Hazelrigg.

Passing a wired enclosure, the path follows the wall above Back Reddings Wood and climbs a little rocky hill towards a square observation tower, a relic of the war. Reaching a recently enlarged pool, where we saw a pair of tufted ducks circling, turn right down through the bracken to Back Reddings Allotment and its extensive 16 acre tarn. This too is a private fishery belonging to Bigland Hall Estate, and is stocked with trout. The numerous small islands are connected to the shore by walkways and there is a long dam to retain the waters of Black Beck. Though completely artificial, for it was made in 1977, we found the tarn reminiscent of Tarn Hows without the trees. The otherwise rather bleak surrounding boggy moorland is brightened by white tufts of cotton-grass, and in the spring by hawthorn blossom.

201

Canny Hill Tarn

The right of way goes along by the wall to a small gate and a signpost where you turn left on the footpath to Hazelrigg. The rough fellside is boggy in places, with small rocky outcrops, scrubby gorse and hawthorn amongst the bracken, and the path is very indistinct. But keep to the left of the wall to reach another signpost, then go through the gate by a sheepfold to join the farm road. The wooded lane leads past a farm to the white-washed cottage of Hazelrigg, and Hazelrigg Lane is joined at the bend.

Turn left past Harebridge House, which has an unusual double gable, then before you reach the wood there is a step stile over the wall. Crossing a beautiful meadow, which has a wide variety of flowers including orchids, the footpath to Backbarrow leads over a step stile into Hoggarth's Plantation. The narrow path in the wood goes along a ride through tall bracken, then kinks right and left to follow a grassy forest track gently up the hill.

Leaving the plantation to emerge into the sunlight at a ladder stile, a narrow trod follows the wall downhill. There is a fine view of the foot of Windermere, framed by Finsthwaite Heights and Gummer's How, then an obvious path is joined at a field gate. To the right, the path leads down towards Newby Bridge, and on the open fellside amid a sea of bracken is Canny Hill Tarn. Surrounded by a wire fence, this former reservoir now has private fishing, but it is scarcely worth the effort of a closer approach.

Backbarrow (*Hill shaped like a back*)

From the gate and heading south-west, the path makes its way gently down the shallow valley in Bishop's Allotment. In the distance is Cartmel Sands, and on a hill above Ulverston is the Hoad Monument, built in memory of Sir John Barrow who was born there in 1764. Sir John, for forty years Secretary of the Admiralty, was a founder of the Royal Geographical Society, and his support of Arctic exploration was marked by the naming of Barrow Strait near the North Pole.

The path peters out in a boggy area, but a faint trod bends right to climb to the little ridge, then crossing a small stream continues in the same direction into pastureland. Many of the rights of way across these hills have disappeared, and there is now little sign of the path, but aim to the left of the cottage, where a ladder stile brings you to the road. Across the valley is the yellow, glazed brick Haverthwaite Station, built in 1872, which is now the terminus of the trains. Once the line linked with Barrow, but these days the trains are confined to $3^{1}/_{2}$ miles of track ending at the Lakeside pier of the Windermere Iron Steamboat Company.

Low Wood

Follow the road downhill and round the bend towards the industrial village of Backbarrow, then turn left along the bridleway. Accompanied by the shrill

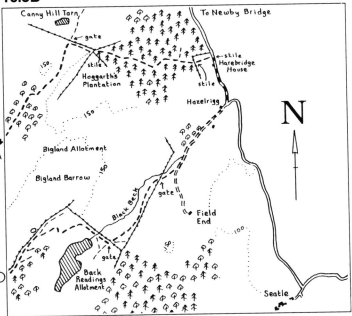

whistles of the steam trains, the bridleway leads through fields fringed in early summer with bistort, creeping buttercup and greater stitchwort, while down in the valley, on the far side of the River Leven, the shortest river in Cumbria, are the remains of the Backbarrow Iron-works. Backbarrow was one of the oldest continuously worked iron-making sites in Britain and only ceased production in 1967.

The path continues through a pretty bluebell wood, strongly garlic scented in spring by the white flowers of ramsons, and below is a mill race which powered the Gunpowder Works at Low Wood. The explosive was made from imported saltpetre and sulphur mixed with locally coppiced charcoal, a highly dangerous occupation, and there were many accidents. Joining the road turn right, past cottages which were once the stable block of the works. The Clock Tower, built in 1849 as the administrative offices, now houses a crystal engraver and a domestic appliance and furniture store.

Opposite the Clock Tower a road leads past a row of attractive cottages to the B5278. The layby is then just uphill, while the railway station is to the right across Low Wood Bridge.

203

WALK 10.4: CARTMEL FELL

Tarns:	Fiddler Hall Tarn
	Simpson Ground Reservoir
	Raven's Barrow Tarn
	Middle Tarn
	Sow How Tarn
	Gummer's How Tarn
Distance:	8¹/₂ miles
Ascent:	1300ft
Summary:	Easy walking on good paths and tracks through fields and woodland with the best ever view of Windermere from Gummer's How.
Starting Point:	(GR 389875) Gummer's How picnic place, 2 miles north-west of Newby Bridge.

Wainwright had finished. His *Pictorial Guide to the Lakeland Fells* was complete and the concluding words of the final volume, penned at Christmas 1965, made it quite clear: "Regretfully I reject suggestions of a Book 8". But nine years later, to everyone's delight, the ban was lifted, and Gummer's How joined a hundred other Outlying Fells as a new and worthy objective. "A little Beauty - a classic view" he enthused, and indeed looking at the Tourist Map there must be something very special about Gummer's How, for it is given the full treatment, a whole 360 degree red star viewpoint, the only one in the area, and surveying over 100 square miles.

Yet Wainwright doesn't mention the tarns of Cartmel Fell. Elsewhere hardly a pool escaped his pen as he recorded the fells of Lakeland, but Gummer's How and the hillside above Staveley-in-Cartmel appear bereft. Only Sow How Tarn is mentioned, and even then it is dismissed as "artificial". Perhaps it's simply a matter of perspective.

When Nathaniel Hawthorn came to the Lakes in the summer of 1855 he wrote of "a lovely little pool among the hills, long and narrow, beautifully indented with tiny bays and headlands". An excellent description of a tarn, but actually he was talking about Windermere. Hawthorn, the first great fiction writer of the United States, had been given a four year consular post in Liverpool, and during his travels filled several notebooks with descriptions of his many sightseeing trips in England: "All the scenery we have met with is in excellent taste, and keeps itself within very proper bounds, never getting too wild and rugged to shock the sensitivities of cultivated people, as American scenery is apt to do".

There were certainly many cultivated people around Windermere. In the nineteenth century Fell Foot was a private house, with a garden of

Sow How Tarn

rhododendrons, oaks and pine trees, a grand estate owned by the former mayor of Leeds, Jeremiah Dixon. His father-in-law, John Smeaton, who built the Eddystone Lighthouse, was a regular visitor, and from the fell tops Nathaniel Hawthorn would have seen the replica of the lighthouse which stands on Hoad Hill above Ulverston, which had just been built as a memorial to Sir John Barrow, Arctic explorer and founder of the Royal Geographical Society. In 1859 Colonel Ridelaugh bought the estate and immediately set about building a series of Gothic castellated boathouses along the water's edge to

form a miniature dockyard for his collection of boats. His 66ft steam yacht the *Fairy Queen* was built on the Clyde and transported here in sections, only to be succeeded by the even larger and more luxurious *Britannia*.

Now owned by the National Trust, Fell Foot is to be restored to some of its former glory. It is too late for the house, demolished in 1907 to make way for an even grander mansion which got no further than the foundations before the new owner died, but the boathouses remain and the gardens are to be restored, creating once again the atmosphere of the Victorian Age.

As we climbed one April morning from Staveley-in-Cartmel up across the open hillside, past the ruins of the old mines and into the woodland, there was no-one about. In the forest the mist hung low, and there was no-one to be seen among the trees on reaching Fiddler Hall Tarn. A solitary walker hurried past us on the track to Simpson Ground, but strolling across the fields to Sow How Tarn the only moving figures in the landscape were sheep. No sounds disturbed Middle Tarn save a solitary moorhen, and even the farms seemed still asleep. Climbing to Gummer's How a couple greeted us cheerily, but on the summit once again we were alone. We had been walking for several hours in the 'overcrowded Lake District' and as we looked down on Windermere, the lake far below seemed little changed since the days of Nathaniel Hawthorn, and the passage of 140 years.

ROUTE DESCRIPTION

Staveley-in-Cartmel (*Wood where staves were got, near the sandbank by the rocky ground*)

From Gummer's How car park, walk down the road along Fell Foot Brow. This is no hardship for the lane is quiet and there is a splendid view of Windermere, busy with small boats, cruisers and passenger steamers, while across the lake are the Haverthwaite steam trains. After ¹/₂ mile, just beyond a forest road, a footpath signed to Staveley goes over a stile into the wood. The little path descends gently across bluebell covered slopes to a step stile over a stone wall. Continuing through the trees past more bluebells the path emerges from the wood at a stile over a fence, where a track leads right, through a gate and between the buildings to the road.

Turning left towards Staveley-in-Cartmel, fork left at the junction, then go left again after the telephone box along the bridleway. Chapel House, after which the woods are named, is a little further along the road past St Mary's church, which unusually for Lakeland has an extension faced with overlapping slate tiles.

Fiddler Hall Tarn

The walled track leads past the houses and through the wood to a gate where you go left into a field. After a boggy patch the bridleway winds its way up the hillside, following a deep grove which has been worn by traffic from old mine workings. Reaching a gate into Chapel House Plantation, the bridleway continues gently uphill, crossing first a rough track and then a forest road. The path continues climbing through the trees, then at the top of the hill the bridleway turns off, but a footpath keeps straight on to join another forest road. The trees soon thin to a larch plantation and Fiddler Hall Tarn lies in the large clearing beyond. Named after a house in the valley below, which now stands on the far side of the busy A590, the tarn is secluded and quiet with a little peninsula and a grassy island, while in the foreground a fallen tree forms a natural seat.

Simpson Ground Reservoir

As the forest road bends left, the right of way turns off down a grassy ride and over Bog End Moss, then continues through the trees to the edge of the forest. Becoming very indistinct over rough pastureland, the path goes

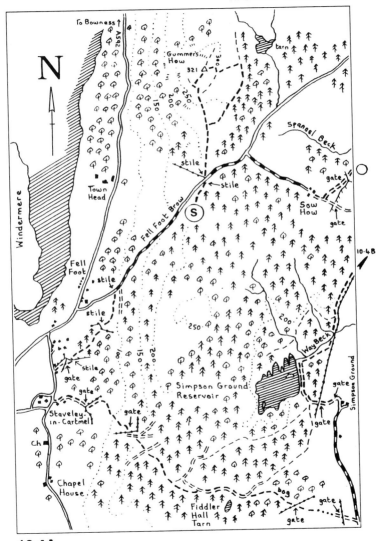

10.4A

through a field gate and on to join a lane where you turn left past a number of cattle grids, all deterringly signed private, to arrive at Simpson Ground. The name dates from the early sixteenth century when the monks of Furness Abbey created new holdings called 'grounds' which were named after the tenant families.

At the road end turn left on the bridleway to Staveley where a little gate leads back into Chapel House Plantation by an ancient notice 'North West Water, No Admittance'. Turning right to the reservoir dam, another decaying notice proclaims 'Keep Out, Moving Machinery, Deep Water'. All very forbidding, but the right of way is waymarked through the woods, which are now part of Grizedale Forest. The water is only used these days as a local backup for the Haweswater aqueduct to Barrow, and as an emergency supply for Grange over Sands. Apart from the dam, Simpson Ground Reservoir blends into the area well, and is a most attractive setting with bracken covered slopes, rocky outcrops and a backdrop of conifers.

Raven's Barrow Tarn (*Raven's hill tarn*)

Keeping beneath the long dam with its hand rail, the footpath turns down through the trees halfway along, though most people seem to stay by the dam and follow Way Beck. Staying to the right of the boggy ground, the path then goes along by the wall and crosses the beck. A footpath joins from the left, but keep beside the wall where there is a wide panorama over the fields towards Whitbarrow.

A wooden stile leads out of the forest, then going through the rocky knolls, the path passes to the right of a solitary Scots pine. The view now opens out over the bracken covered slopes of Raven's Barrow to the flat, green Vale of Winster and the long limestone ridge of Whitbarrow.

A shallow indentation marks the line of the grassy path across the field, then joining a farm track you turn right through a gate and past the houses at Foxfield. Just after the bend, leave the tarmac road and turn left through a gate onto a footpath across the field. In 200 yards the path turns sharp right through a gate onto a walled track, and then you continue in the same direction through the scattered trees of Gateside Plantation.

After crossing a meandering beck, a footpath forks off left and climbs gently through the bracken to a deer fence, where humans climb the ladder stile, but dogs have their own special gate. A narrow belt of tall Scots pine protects the new larch plantation, where fortunately some of the old native hardwoods remain. The quiet little tarn, which lies to the right of the path, well screened by the trees and fringed with bulrushes and irises, is a relatively new creation for it is not marked on the OS map.

Middle Tarn

The path keeps straight on past some ancient yews to a ladder stile, then

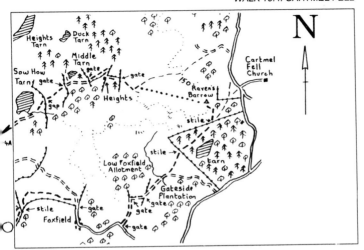

10.4B

leaving the right of way, which leads to the ancient chapel of St Anthony, you fork left and climb the little path which slants up the hillside. On the fell top is a slate column fashioned as a sheltered seat, though it only accommodates small people, and there is a splendid 180 degree panorama to the east from this delightful grass and rock studded summit.

Heading westwards along the fell top, an indistinct grassy track is joined in about ¼ mile which leads to a gate at the corner of a plantation. The track continues beside the rhododendrons and past the ruined Heights Cottage. Used as a Quaker Meeting House until the 1920s, this was built in 1667 to comply with the Five Mile Act, which prevented a Non-conformist preacher from living or teaching within 5 miles of a town. The track then climbs round the corner of a wood to enter the trees.

Just before you come out of the wood a path detours right to Middle Tarn along a tunnel in the rhododendrons, and as we emerged from the undergrowth, a startled heron rose into the air. The tarn, which is now only about half its original size, is very overgrown with bottle sedge, rhododendrons shade the water and the wooden jetty is slowly rotting away.

Sow How Tarn

Returning to the bridleway continue through the gate and along a little rocky ridge. The track goes down to the left of the attractive Sow How Tarn to cross a fast-flowing stream. This very grand tarn has a stone boathouse topped by a weather vane, and standing by the low stone-faced retaining dam we saw several fish leaping from the water.

Gummer's How

The track is followed across fields, where on a grey April morning there was no-one about, but the little lambs were a delight. Turn right at the junction to Sow How Farm and follow Sow How Lane along the edge of Astley's Plantation, then turn left along the road. Over the brow of the hill and in about 250 yards, a footpath is signed 'to Gummer's How Summit Only'.

The ascent is deceptive and doesn't take long for there is less than 400ft of climbing. A final rocky scramble leads to the top of this little fell which is a mountain in miniature. From the summit trig point, at just over a thousand feet the highest point of Cartmel Fell, there is a magnificent view. Esthwaite Water, Sow How Tarn, and the full length of Windermere are on show, the Hoad Monument, which has links with Fell Foot, lies to the south-west, while in the woods below to the north-east, the final tarn of the walk can be seen.

Gummer's How Tarn

Take the little path which heads north-eastwards straight for the tarn and then turn right above Gummer's How Plantation. Though the surroundings are private there is a good view through the trees of this secluded man-made tarn, which is really a disused reservoir.

Follow the path along the edge of the plantation, then at the corner of the wood, head towards the foot of Windermere. The main path is rejoined, and retracing your steps to the road you go through a kissing gate to the picnic area and car park.

WALK 10.5: WHITBARROW

Tarns:	Toby Tarn
	Argles Tarn
	Witherslack Hall Tarn
Distance:	4 miles
Ascent:	750ft
Summary:	Two tiny limestone tarns are the excuse for this climb to the summit of Whitbarrow, which is seen at its best in early summer.
Starting Point:	(GR 430872) Minor road 2 miles north of Witherslack. Off road parking at the beginning of the walk.

Limestone pavement on Whitbarrow Scar

To the south-west of Kendal, between the Lyth valley and the even quieter River Winster, rises the great ridge of Whitbarrow. High white cliffs tower above steep scree slopes covered in hazel and ash woodland, and on the summit is a Nature Reserve. This is a countryside beloved of botanists, for unlike central Lakeland, where many of the flowers are only to be found clinging to inaccessible mountain ledges, here on Whitbarrow the whole hillside is limestone and a paradise for plants.

Limestone is not a rock that many people associate with the Lake District, for the Central Fells are volcanic in origin, while the more rounded shapes of Skiddaw and the Northern Fells are sedimentary slate. But during the Carboniferous Period, some 300 million years ago, the whole of the Lake District was covered with limestone. There were no hills then, just a warm shallow sea where coral reefs grew, and as countless millions of tiny shells settled to the bottom, so the limestone rock was formed. Though earth movement later lifted up the area into a huge dome, most of the limestone has since been eroded away, but here, in south-east Lakeland, is a remnant of that ancient coral sea.

The summit of Whitbarrow is an even bigger surprise for on Lord's Seat is a magnificent stretch of limestone pavement. Smooth, rounded, water-worn rock, split and fissured into clints and grikes, shelters plants including hart's tongue fern, wood sage, herb Robert, and maidenhair spleenwort. The surface of the rock, looking as clean and new as when it was scraped bare during the Ice Age, stays that way simply because, unlike most rock which weathers to produce soil, the limestone is so pure it dissolves to leave nothing behind.

After a steep climb through the woods, where coppiced stools of hazel trees are reminders of an industrial past, we emerged onto the open fell top. The cowslips and wood anemones were over, but massed in bloom were the delicate golden tissue-paper flowers of rock roses, while among the short turf grew thyme, fairy flax and bird's foot trefoil. The heather is a bit of a surprise, for this is a plant of acid moorland, but thousands of years of rain have leached the nutrients from the soil to leave a surface speckled with tormentil, while other plants root deeper to tap the underlying lime.

Crossing the open fell we came to Toby Tarn. It isn't much, just a small patch of clear silver among the thickly growing sedge, and were it anywhere else the tarn would remain anonymous and unvisited, but here it is a rarity on a hillside which will be remembered for its flowers.

On the grassland are pale blue harebells, dusky red salad burnett and frothy yellow lady's bedstraw, while on the eastern slopes of the hill the common spotted orchid grows tall and vigorous. There is bugle, self heal and the lemon-scented fern, whose tall tapering fronds when crushed between the fingers have a tangy smell, while spread thickly on the rocks around the summit cairn is that brilliant yellow fleshy-leaved plant, the biting stonecrop.

In the woods we found lily-of-the-valley, while among the scrubland, to our delight, were the newly opened buds of the dark red heleborine.

The walk was almost over as we came down the road past Witherslack Hall Tarn, worthy indeed of the name with its lovely water-lilies, and we wondered if we would again see a Roe deer. But the animal that burst out of the trees was no shy wild thing, for suddenly into the road smartly trotted a horse. Attached to its harness by a chain trailed a log, a whole tree in fact. The horse, and his two companions waiting patiently beside a growing pile of timber, belonged to three foresters who told us they also worked in Grizedale, Whinlatter and the Levens Estate. "They enjoy the work" said one of the men, patting the horse standing proudly beside its pile of logs. And with its sleek coat steaming in the cool afternoon air, it seemed thoroughly happy, and in no doubt that this was one of the best jobs in the world.

ROUTE DESCRIPTION

Toby Tarn

The right of way to Whitbarrow follows a track into the mossy wood, through hazel and silver birch once coppiced for charcoal, and then begins to climb. In about half a mile, at a junction, the stony path bends right and then in a few yards left, to continue steeply up the limestone scree through woodland with many ancient yews. Reaching a kissing gate the path enters Flodder Allotment, a Nature Reserve which was created in 1962, and climbing on, emerges onto the open fell top with fine views back over Winster Vale and Cartmel Fell. To the right is the entrance of a trial level, driven in the middle of the eighteenth century in the quest for lead.

Staying near the wall, with to the left a fine stone man, a cross wall is reached, and a stone step stile by a gate leads to Toby Tarn. Limestone outcrops slope down to the edge, where there are large patches of butterwort whose rosettes of sticky leaves enfold unsuspecting insects, but little more than a large boggy hollow with only a few small patches of open water, Toby Tarn does not really deserve its grand title.

Argles Tarn (*Named after a local family*)

A ladder stile crosses back over the wall into Horse Pasture Wood, then after 400 yards, at a cairned junction, you turn right uphill. Beside the path grow the tall narrow yellow-green fronds of the lemon-scented fern. Joining another path in an area of limestone pavement, the climb continues to a stile back into the Hervey Nature Reserve. Go left, following a low limestone escarpment, and when the path turns uphill keep beside the limestone outcrops past large clumps of juniper. Bundles of juniper cut from this fell were used when the turnpike from Greenodd to Levens, now the busy A590, was made in 1820 to 'float' the new road across the boggy land beside the estuary.

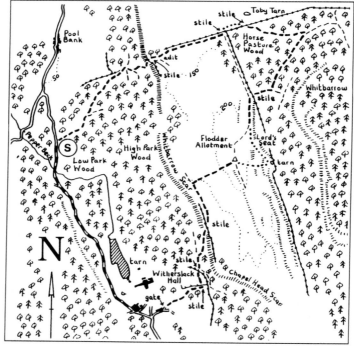

10.5

Heading towards the wall the second little tarn is soon reached, another boggy hollow, almost completely overgrown with bottle sedge and fed by springs of clear water. The autumn gentian, which can be found here, was popular with seventeenth-century herbalists and was named after King Gentius of Illyria who discovered its medicinal uses. Though very small, it is surprising that these high limestone tarns are here at all, for the rock is nearly pure calcium carbonate, which dissolves on weathering, and consequently is not much good for holding water.

Lord's Seat

After a short climb westwards over an intervening small ridge, and skirting an area of limestone pavement bounded by low cliffs, the summit cairn on Lord's Seat is reached. Built on the highest point of Whitbarrow, it commemorates the founder of the Lake District Naturalists' Trust, Canon G.A.K. Hervey. From here the northern half of the compass is a semicircle of distant mountains, and southwards is Morecambe Bay. Before the new turnpike road was built, the main route to the Lakes was over the sands of the estuary. The Carter family acted as guides and a gentleman crossing from Lancaster asked if Carters were never lost on the sands? "I never knew any lost" said the guide, "there's one or two drowned now and then, but they're generally somewhere i'th bed when th'tide goes out".

Witherslack Hall Tarn (*Wooded valley hall tarn*)

Westwards, a cairned path leads down to the top of Whitbarrow Scar where Witherslack Hall can be seen half-hidden in the trees below. Turning left the path descends gently to a stile in the wall, then slants dramatically down through coppiced woodland across the face of the scar. The high cliffs on the escarpment are used by climbers, but they are not allowed on the crags during the bird-nesting season.

Leaving the trees the path skirts a football pitch to join a track past farm buildings to the road. Turn right along the tarmac past Witherslack Hall School, which can be seen through the trees, and the tarn comes into view. Surrounded by unfenced woodland and really more of an ornamental lake, though it was built as a fish pond, the tarn has a small boathouse, the banks are fringed with yellow iris and in summer white water-lilies float on the surface. It is then about ½ mile back to the start of the walk along the quiet lane through the trees, where if you are lucky you may glimpse a Roe deer.

Rock roses

11: South-Eastern Tarns

WALK 11.1: BOWNESS

Tarns:	School Knott Tarn
	Borwick Fold Tarn
	Cleabarrow Tarn
Distance:	5 miles
Ascent:	350ft
Summary:	A good walk for the spring, with easy walking along paths and unfenced lanes.
Starting Point:	(GR 424962) Roadside parking by Windermere golf course on the B5824.

It was a wet day. The kind of thoroughly wet grey day when it hardly seems to get light, the rain comes down steadily and relentlessly, running off trees and roofs, with great heavy wet drops splashing in the puddles, and every surface is alive with little streams. The sort of day when you know it isn't going to let up for hours, perhaps not at all, and the thought of a walk was not appealing. School Knott Tarn would have to wait. Instead we went to see the boats.

Now for a lover of boats, or even anyone with a passing interest in them, Windermere Steamboat Museum is a treasure house. Steamers, motorboats and sailing dinghies; engines, propellers and oars; pictures of boats and models of boats, while during the summer the museum comes alive when visitors are taken out on Windermere.

Captain John of *Swallows and Amazons* would perhaps not have approved, as motorboats were "for the people who did not know how to manage sails", but even he would have been impressed by *Brankson*. Admiring the teak and walnut, glistening new with the sheen of varnish, it seems incredible that she was constructed in 1896. *Otto* was built in the same year, and the two of them, berthed in the indoor harbour, are a delight. Even older is a steam launch built in 1850 and oldest of all is a sailing yacht of 1780, but the flat-bottomed little barge, which we expected to be told had been raised from the bottom of the lake and dated back to the Vikings, proved to be the boat in which Beatrix Potter rowed on Moss Eccles Tarn.

Windermere or Winander Mere as it was once known, probably comes from the Norse 'Vinander's Mere', but the town is a latecomer, a creation of the railway, now expanded out of all recognition from the former village of Birthwaite. The Windermere Hotel was built in 1847 when the railway opened, and by the 1880s there were 40 lodging houses. Wordsworth campaigned vigorously against the coming of the railway with letters to the *Morning Post* and a sonnet which began "Is then no nook of English ground secure From rash assault?", but being also a businessman he later bought shares in the venture.

It was still raining as later that afternoon we put on boots and waterproofs, and still raining as we squelched up the track towards School Knott Tarn. There was little to see in the mist, just tiny wavelets splashing on the shore, and we walked on across the grassy knoll of School Knott, and into the dripping trees beyond. Woods, even in rain, cheer the spirits, and tea was eaten beside the flowers of wood sorrel and wood anemones, folded up tight against the deluge, surrounded by carpets of bright yellow-green velvety moss.

In the fields beyond, the cows looked solemnly at us, their wet noses glistening in the rain, and as we reached the car and peeled off our soggy clothing it was still raining, but we had enjoyed the walk. And if we can enjoy the tarns in the rain, how much more they will be enjoyed on that perfect sunny day we hope you have!

Wood Anemonies

ROUTE DESCRIPTION
School Knott Tarn

From the corner of the main road take the Dales Way, which is signposted along the narrow tarmac lane. Cleabarrow Tarn, surrounded by rushes and with a small wooded island, sits in the field to the right, but there is a better view of it on the way back. Passing High Cleabarrow, with its round Westmorland chimneys, the road becomes a gated track and continues through the fields past a newly planted copse. After crossing a beck the track doubles back at a junction to climb the hill to a kissing gate. The Dales Way now sets off on its 80 mile journey to Yorkshire, so leaving it you follow the left side of the wall to School Knott Tarn. This long narrow tarn, overlooked by a handful of conifers, is entirely natural, and its clear water is fished for trout by the Windermere and Ambleside District Angling Association.

Borwick Fold Tarn (*Corn farm field tarn*)

There is little sign on the ground of the right of way, but going left up to the kissing gate in the wall, it is an easy stroll north-west across the grass to the top of School Knott. Though the rocky knoll is only 761 ft high there is a grand panorama of the mountains beyond Windermere. The Coniston Fells, Scafell Pike, Bow Fell and the Langdale Pikes are all on show, while to the north lie the Kentmere Fells. School Knott is said by Wainwright "to give the finest view of the town" but the foreground is marred by the large housing estate at Heathwaite, which was built as a 'workers' suburb'.

The path leads down to another kissing gate, but don't go through, instead turn right to join a tractor track into Schoolknott Plantation. The footpath becomes more definite as it enters the trees and continues through the bracken to a not very obvious stile in the wall. Crossing a little stream, the path wends its way through scattered larches and over a field to join a tarmac track at a gate. Keeping straight on past Whasdike Farm, don't go over the stile but follow the bridleway beside the wall to a gate where a track leads into the wood. Woods are at their best in the spring and this one is full of anemones, primroses, bluebells, and the strong garlic-smelling ramsons whose pretty white globe-shaped flowers were once used to flavour food.

Crossing a field the bridleway reaches a tarmac lane, where you turn right past High Fairbank Farm. The unfenced road leads over the hill, then turning right again at the T-junction, passes Borwick Fold Tarn. Though the surroundings are private, from the road you can see the tarn and the stone walled dam. It was made by the farmer in the 1930s and a small stone platform has been constructed for fishermen.

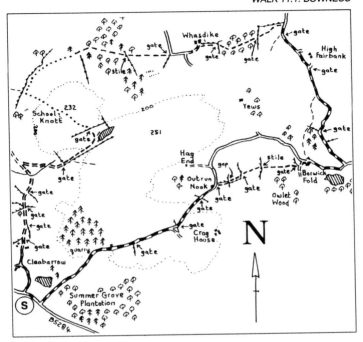

11.1

Cleabarrow Tarn

Immediately after the whitewashed houses of Borwick Fold, once an inn for the men who led the trains of pack ponies, a bridleway turns off to the left, then forking right through a kissing gate, a footpath goes down the middle of the field to a step stile in the wall. Cross to another stile by a gate, then continue round by the wall and through a gap, to join the road at Outrun Nook where you meet the Dales Way again. This time cross straight over the long distance path, and turning left, follow the gated road across the fields, and down by a quarry in a wood, to join the main road. The lane gives a good view of Cleabarrow Tarn, which is now a coarse fishery, stocked by the Angling Association that fly fish at School Knott Tarn.

WALK 11.2: WINSTER VALE

Tarns:	Ghyll Head Fish Pond
	Rosthwaite Farm Tarns
	Stonehills Tarn (Barrow Plantation Tarn)
	Knipe Tarn
	Podnet Tarn (Birket Houses Tarn)
	Ghyll Head Reservoir
Distance:	7½ miles
Ascent:	850ft
Summary:	Easy walking on quiet lanes and tracks round Winster.
Starting Point:	(GR 399925) Roadside parking by Ghyll Head Reservoir, 3 miles south of Bowness.

We were lucky to find it. Only a couple of miles from the honeypot of Windermere, the village of Winster is hidden in a quiet unspoilt valley that seems little changed since the eighteenth century. We could have arrived by horse, for the attractive, ancient, thick-walled house proclaimed that such travellers and their mounts were welcome. In fact Winster is still the sort of place where arrival by horse would be considered the most natural thing in the world. In the doorway the dog did his duty by barking fiercely, then retired inside. We were hardly worth bothering about.

"I usually only take people for one night" confided our hostess, "then if I don't like them, I don't have to put up with them for long". Not sure whether we fitted this category, we were relieved to be offered a cup of tea. "Or would you prefer a beer?" interjected her husband in welcome endorsement of our acceptance, and the rest of a pleasant evening was spent discussing local news, the famous clockmaker who once lived in the house and our favourite subject, the tarns of Lakeland.

In the late seventeenth century Jonas Barber lived in Winster, building clocks in a barn which he used as a workshop. There seems to be some confusion about the Barber family for there were two, or even possibly three generations, all called Jonas, and it is not exactly clear which of them was the famous clockmaker, but a longcase clock made by Barber still ticks sonorously in the hall.

Winster is well supplied with tarns, but one of the most attractive came as a surprise to us. "Have you been to Podnet?" enquired the man we met near Winster House. We had not, and for a very good reason it was missing from our map. Somehow the Ordnance Survey had forgotten about Podnet Tarn. It was there in 1972, but on the 1982 edition of the map Podnet Tarn had vanished as though it never was.

The day was sunny but cold, a proper wintry spell of weather, and Podnet

Tarn was frozen. Frozen solid right across, it gleamed in the low sunlight, and slowly circling the ice, keeping to the edge where it was thickest and strongest, were two skaters. Their breath steamed in the still air, a faint swishing sound came from the steel blades, while graceful curving lines showed their tracks across the ice.

"Would you like a go?" offered the charming man who glided up to us, then as he and his wife took off their skates he told us that he worked at the Freshwater Biological Association. An engineer by training rather than a biologist, one of his responsibilities was negotiating with landowners for access to the tarns and lakes.

Skaters on Podnet Tarn

THE TARNS OF LAKELAND VOL.2: EAST

There are few lowland tarns left in the Lake District that are untouched and we were content to add Ghyll Head Reservoir to our list, but the intriguing thing about it was the windmill. Floating on a platform in the middle of the tarn, its arms turned slowly in the breeze. Driving a pump, it was lifting water from the depths of the tarn to create a circulating flow, discouraging the growth of the dreaded blue-green algae.

It is only, in the words of the experts, 'productive' lakes that suffer with blue-green algae, ones where the water has become enriched by an influx of organic matter and fertiliser. Lakes such as Wast Water, being surrounded by hard rocks rather than agricultural land, are fortunately immune, but every summer Windermere and Esthwaite Water, and many reservoirs too, are prone to algal bloom. However enrichment by fertiliser is only part of the story. There has been concern in recent years about acid rain and its effect on fish. Much research has been carried out at Ferry House by the Freshwater Biologists, and over in the Duddon valley an experiment is currently in progress where they are adding fertiliser to Seathwaite Tarn to promote the growth of algae and neutralise the effect of acid rain. It's a delicate balance. Let's hope they get it right.

ROUTE DESCRIPTION
Ghyll Head Fish Pond

Opposite the end of the reservoir a permissive path leads into the Ghyll Head Access Area. Follow this through the wood and round the bend, then just before a little rocky outcrop, a narrow trod goes off to the left. Reaching the boundary of the Access Land you get a good view of Ghyll Head Fish Pond, which is in the private grounds of a house. Shaded by larch trees, with its surface patterned by lily pads, this old reservoir is retained by an artificial dam.

Rosthwaite Farm Tarns (*Clearing with a heap of stones*)

Returning to the permissive path, continue through the trees, then crossing a couple of wooden step stiles follow the edge of the plantation. At another step stile the path comes out onto the open fell and a track is joined at a signposted junction with a fine view along Windermere to the Fairfield Horseshoe and Red Screes beyond.

Turn right on the track across Rosthwaite Allotment, where the rocky banks are covered with yellow tormentil, the tiny white flowers of heath bedstraw and dark gentian-blue milkwort, and keep straight on at a junction to a field gate and past Rosthwaite Farm. In the sandy yard is a horse walker, a dovecote complete with doves, and everywhere is neat and tidy, while to complete the scene the owners have constructed their own private tarn fringed with fishing platforms, where a sad-looking plastic heron stands as a deterrent to the real thing.

222

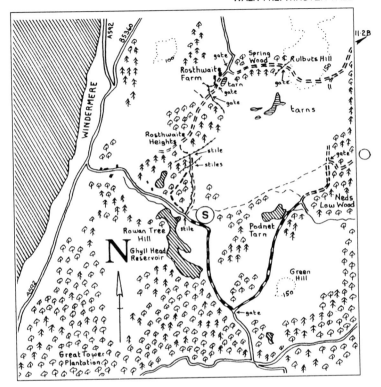

11.2A

Immediately after the farm the footpath to Winster turns right through the larch plantation of Spring Wood. The track climbs gently across the slopes of Rulbuts Hill, where a rocky knoll covered with the pink stars of English stonecrop overlooks a large shallow tarn surrounded by shooting hides. These tarns at Rosthwaite Farm are not shown on the OS map, though they have been here at least fifteen years.

Stonehills Tarn

As the path crosses the brow of the hill, the scattered houses of Winster appear ahead. Once it was planned to flood this valley to provide a reservoir, but mercifully Winster Vale has been spared.

Passing a stone walled enclosure with an ancient yew, a track is joined which continues down the hill, then where it bends away to High House, keep straight on through the field gate. There is little sign of the bridleway which has fallen into disuse, but keeping near the ruined wall continue down to a field gate into the wood. An old slate slab bridges the stream which is then followed along the shady green lane, and out through the garden of a renovated cottage to the road.

Winster was the birthplace in 1780 of William Pearson, naturalist, poet and friend of Wordsworth, and to the right is the seventeenth-century Compston House, which until recently was the post office. They breed them tough in Winster, for in 1692 the church steeple "fell upon a Sunday morning in time of Service, and some of the stones fell upon Ann Comston but she was not harmed".

Turning left, leave Winster and walk up to the main road. Crossing straight over, continue up the single track road, then at the next crossroads turn right along Green Lane past Stonehills whose gate is topped by a solemn stone owl. The track becomes unsurfaced and climbs the hill by Barrow Plantation to cross the open fell. Stonehills Tarn, which is private, is now in view with its little jetty, an island with a tall tree, and a small wood.

Knipe Tarn (Tarn by the steep overhanging rock)

Green Lane, its banks golden with broom in early summer, continues to climb between old stone walls. The verges are full of bluebells, aromatic wood sage, the frothy white flowers of pignut, little pink bells of bilberry and even some heather. The hard fern, which grows here, is one of the few ferns to remain green all year, and is readily recognised in summer by its growth of separate, narrower fertile fronds.

The track crosses Undermillbeck Common which has at least half a dozen tarns, but despite its title of 'common' the public are denied access. However from near the highest point on the lane you may be able to glimpse one in a hollow to the south. Joining the road turn right and keep right at the fork to view Knipe Tarn, which though it is private is well seen from the road through its screen of trees. The large tarn, which has a wooded island where swans nest, is retained by a stone dam at the far end near the house.

Winster (Stream on the left)

Retrace your steps to the road junction, then turn right and follow the lane downhill with pleasant views into the valley towards Crook. The name means bend in the river, and it was at Crook that John Braithwaite invented the bobbin-making machine that revolutionised the industry. Keep straight on at the corner, along twin strips of tarmac with flower filled verges, then fork right by a barn and through a gate. Beneath the wooded escarpment of Bow Mabble Breast, the bridleway climbs to a kissing gate, then descends gently

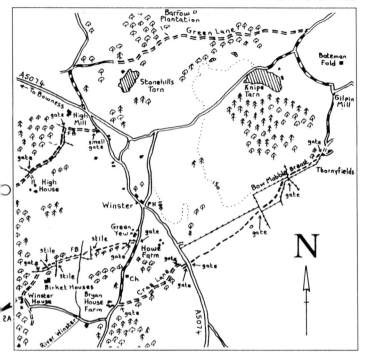

11.2B

past a marshy pool, used for wildfowling, which is overgrown with bogbean and yellow irises.

Crossing straight over the road the bridleway goes across a meadow to a gate onto Crag Lane. Fording the stream by a little slate slab footbridge, the track climbs over the hill and down to join the road at Bryan Houses, the home of Winster's famous clockmaker. Turn right past Holy Trinity church, a simple slate building which was constructed in 1875 to replace an earlier seventeenth-century chapel. A bell, the font and some oval painted texts are all that remain of the ancient church, described as "whitewashed both inside and out".

Podnet Tarn

Follow the lane towards Winster and turn left just before Green Yew Farm over the stone step stile. After a complicated old-fashioned gate, complete with instructions, the path goes down the edge of the wood to a step stile across the fence, and into the field. The grandly named Jubilee Bridge, with its awkward metal rails, crosses the River Winster, once the boundary between Westmorland and Lancashire, then climbing beside the wall, you cross the fields by a couple of step stiles to join the track which passes Birket Houses. Though this mansion appears very old, it was actually built in 1910, replacing a medieval ruin which stood to the right of the path.

The track leads to the Georgian Winster House where you turn uphill by the large barn, along a green lane through the trees. Reaching a kissing gate turn left and follow the track round the perimeter of Neds Low Wood to join the tarmac lane from Low House. Podnet Tarn, now reinstated on the map by the Ordnance Survey, is fringed with bogbean and bulrushes, water-lilies bloom in summer and swans nest on the far bank. It was constructed as a shooting tarn and the fishing is private with strict instructions to return all fish caught.

Ghyll Head Reservoir

From the grassy knoll beside the lane there is a wide panorama of the high Lakeland Fells. The Coniston Fells, the Langdale Pikes, Helvellyn, the Fairfield Horseshoe and High Street are all in view, while to the south Winster Vale continues towards the sea. Passing the raised bog of Birket Houses Allotment where we have seen Roe deer grazing, the road is reached and you turn right past Great Tower Plantation. The wood is a favourite with orienteers as well as with the scouts to whom it was presented in 1936. Soon Ghyll Head Reservoir appears. Though obviously artificial, the reservoir which once supplied Windermere with drinking water, and is now used only as an emergency top-up, looks pleasant enough, set between green fields and the plantation, but there is no access except for members of the Windermere Ambleside and District Angling Association, who fish for rainbow trout. It is then a pleasant walk back up the road to end the walk, with a distant view of the Langdale Pikes.

WALK 11.3: RATHER HEATH AND CUNSWICK SCAR

Tarns:	Ratherheath Tarn
	Ratherheath Tarn Small (Scream Point)
	Cunswick Tarn
	Moss Side Tarn
Distance:	5 miles
Ascent:	450ft
Summary:	Easy walking along unfrequented paths.

Starting Point: (GR 485958) Ratherheath Lane, off the A591 3 miles north-west of Kendal. Roadside parking by the tarn.

To the north-west of Kendal are two quiet and apparently unassuming lowland tarns. However, things are not always what they seem, for Cunswick Tarn and Ratherheath Tarn have not only royal connections, but sex and violence too.

The association of Cunswick Tarn with Henry VIII is perhaps obvious, for it was at Cunswick Hall that the king stayed while courting his sixth and last wife, Katherine Parr, but the link with sex is generally less well known. Henry was seeking a new wife, and though Katherine, who was born at Kendal Castle, had already outlived two husbands, she was pretty, she was wealthy and she was a widow, and it was a widow that Henry was looking for.

Henry's fifth marriage had ended disastrously. It had been discovered that the queen, Catherine Howard, was not the pure maiden Henry believed her to be when they were married and there had been at least two other men in her life. Not only did several female servants know of this, some of them had even spent the night with Catherine and her lovers!

When Henry learned of his wife's past "he remained a long time speechless and at last burst into tears". His skill in "distinguishing a true maid", of which he had boasted when he married Anne of Cleves, had failed him.

Though poor Catherine insisted that she had never been unfaithful, Henry did not believe her and placed an extraordinary law before Parliament stating that any woman the king married would be guilty of treason if she were not a true maid and concealed this fact from the king. Treason was of course punishable by death, so Henry was now looking for a replacement. The people thought this most amusing and Henry was jokingly advised to "espouse a widow!" next time.

Henry's marriage to his new wife Katherine Parr took place on 12th July 1543, and Katherine was fortunate in that she managed to outlive Henry. She even made a fourth marriage, but sadly died soon after giving birth to her first child. Henry's wives are rather confusing but there is a useful little rhyme to remember them by: *Divorced, beheaded, died - divorced, beheaded, survived!*

Rather Heath, which contributes the violence to the story, also has royal connections, for here in 1610 a group of 'statesmen' met to defend their ancient rights against James I. Following the Union of Scotland and England, the Border counties had become both peaceful and prosperous, but the new king, due to what he claimed were "unavoidable expenses", already owed £300,000. With three courts to support, the Royal Navy and sundry other matters, James was rapidly getting into serious debt.

Before the Union, when frequent Scottish raids had demanded a ready army, the farmers who lived in the borders had been granted the freehold of

Ratherheath Tarn

their land in exchange for providing men and arms when needed. But now James I claimed the land was his, declaring that the landowners were mere tenants and should pay rent to the Crown.

The rebel yeomen were ready to fight for their estates and gathered on Rather Heath to present a petition. However on hearing that they were well armed, James had second thoughts and deeming it prudent to look elsewhere for his money, persuaded Parliament to settle for an annual salary of £200,000.

The problems of the present monarchy seem quite trivial by comparison, and nowadays the only people who gather on Rather Heath are fishermen, and their only armaments are rods and nets - but sex is another matter!

ROUTE DESCRIPTION
Ratherheath Tarn (*Tarn on the top of the edge*)
The walk starts on the road beside the large wooded tarn, and though there is a fisherman's path, there is no public access to the water's edge, where wooden platforms jut out from among the rhododendrons. Ratherheath Tarn, like those on Potter Fell, belongs to the Cropper family of Burneside and can be seen from the road.

Ratherheath Tarn Small
Walking westwards on Ratherheath Lane a detour out and back along the public footpath to the right, signed A591, leads across the fields, past the north-western end of Ratherheath Tarn, where we found the marsh cinquefoil. This rather gloomy overgrown pool lies concealed among the trees beyond its larger companion.

Cunswick Tarn
Returning to Ratherheath Lane the route continues past a campsite to the busy Crook Road at Bonning Gate. The word 'gate' indicates that this was once a Roman road and the nearby Cold Harbour Farm, which means shelter, is another sign that the Romans were here. Turn right along the main road for a few yards then go left down Capplerigg Lane.

In about ½ mile, and just before the bungalow, there is a footpath through the field gate to the left. Follow the fence along, and in the rough ground to the left is a pool which is not marked on the OS map. Keep by the wall to a gate, then follow the farm track between the buildings of Fell Gate, another Roman connection.

A rough track heads east through the field to a gate, and the next field is crossed diagonally, aiming just to the right of the mast on the skyline. Going through a small enclosure, a long, thin field follows, and towards the far end the path goes through a squeeze stile on the left. After following the hedge, the path slants up through the bushes to cut across the field corner and over

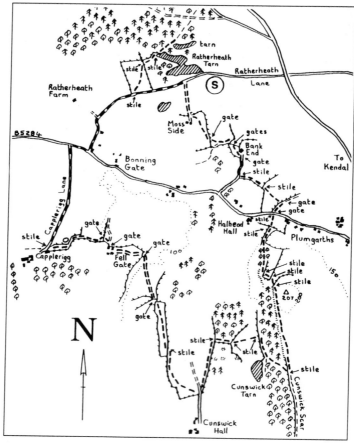

11.3

the drive of Cunswick Hall. This was the home of the Leyburne family in the
fourteenth century and it still has a fifteenth-century gatehouse with the
Royal Arms carved above the gateway, a memento of Henry VIII's visit.

Turning left, follow the wall along past a plantation and by the 'pillow
mounds', probably the remains of a Viking fortification built around the tenth
century. A stile leads into Ash Spring Wood then a field is crossed to a kissing

Bank End

gate. The path now leads along the edge of Scar Wood, and to the right lies Cunswick Tarn. This large stretch of water beneath Cunswick Scar is attractively fringed with rushes and irises. Several pairs of mallards patrolled the surface on our last visit and on the banks were clumps of primroses.

Cunswick Scar

The right of way slopes up through the wood over mossy limestone blocks to a kissing gate onto the mile-long escarpment of Cunswick Scar. This grassy hilltop is very reminiscent of the Derbyshire Dales and in spring and summer is carpeted with lime-loving flowers including dropwort, a close relative of the fragrant meadowsweet. The scar is reputed to be haunted by the ghost of one of the Leyburnes who died for the Catholic faith in Elizabethan times.

Following the cliff edge the distant views ahead are of the Kentmere Fells, westward are the giants of southern Lakeland, and from the large cairn, which marks the highest point of the scar at 679ft, Kendal is in view. To the north-east are the rounded Howgill Fells, while the hills to the east are in Yorkshire.

Moss Side Tarn

Crossing a stile, and then going across a narrow field, the path slants down the hillside through the trees and out to the busy B5824. Go straight across, then turn left through the first gate and cross to a stone step stile in the opposite corner to the left of the trees. The path continues along the field boundary and the lane to Bank End is joined at another stile.

The footpath goes below the house through what appears to be part of the garden, and across the corner of the next field to a gate, then left along the hedge. Going through a field gate, bear right past Moss Side, the house after which the tarn is named, to join the track. Moss Side Tarn, which is over to the left, is very overgrown, a favourite spot of raucous black-headed gulls, and not the most exciting of tarns, though a few white water-lilies remain to enliven the scene in summer. The track then leads out to Ratherheath Lane and Ratherheath Tarn where the walk began.

WALK 11.4: ATKINSON TARN

Tarn:	Atkinson Tarn
Distance:	3 miles
Ascent:	300ft
Summary:	Gentle walking on field paths to an old church and a new fishing tarn.
Starting Point:	(GR 453952) St Catherine's church, Crook. Small layby on B5284 at start of walk. Extra parking by Crook Memorial Hall.

With half a dozen sheets of water, including a named tarn, shown on the map, the hamlet of Crook appeared to be a good place for a walk, so dressed suitably in shorts and tee-shirts, we set off through the fields one sunny June morning. We had progressed no more than a hundred yards when we were attacked.

The *Collins Guide to Insects* informs us that of the 3,500 species of horse-fly to be found in the world, some 160 live in this country. Ours was the cleg-fly, "one of the commonest horse-flies and a real nuisance to man". Supplying further detail the book continues: "Approaches silently" and adds, "Eyes fairly hairy". We hadn't noticed the eyes, but during the next half-hour, first one, then the other exclaimed as yet another silent enemy approached and sunk its teeth into any exposed flesh. It was too much. Despite the now scorching sun we wrapped ourselves in shirts and trousers, even contemplating for a moment wearing gloves, before resuming our search for the tarns.

The Crook tarns proved a disappointment. Of the seven shown on the map, four are private and inaccessible, while the other three. including the

St Catherine's Tower

named Bolton's Tarn, are dried up and simply not worth visiting. Actually Bolton's Tarn is private too, but though the helpful farmer said it would be all right to go, he added "it's not worth looking at", and he's right. With clegs and dried-up tarns, you may be wondering why this walk has appeared in the book, but the reasons are three-fold and the first is St Catherine's Church Tower. Built in about 1620, this is all that remains of the old church, demolished because of structural defects in 1887, and it is a striking piece of architecture, standing isolated in the middle of the fields.

The second and most crucial reason is Atkinson Tarn. It doesn't appear on the map, at least not yet, because it has only recently been constructed. But this fishing lake, visited by swans and mallard, has matured surprisingly quickly and, fringed with irises and yellow water-lilies, is a very pleasant addition to the area.

And the flowers are the third reason for the walk, as strolling through the fields on our second visit, just as hay-making was about to start, we passed meadows full of golden buttercups, tufted vetch, and that most lovely of all the daisies, the ox-eye, while meadow sweet and clover scented the air.

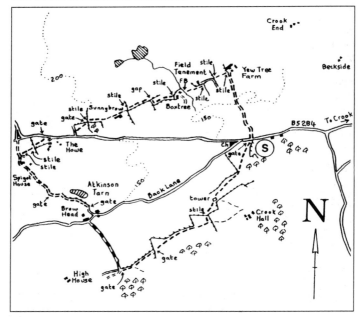

11.4

Bumble bees investigated the remaining foxgloves, the great globular feathery heads of goat's beard were ready to fly in the breeze, and in the hedgerows the delicate starry flowers of lesser stitchwort mingled with greater burnet and the brilliant purple-red spikes of betony. For the colours and scents of the flowers it is worth braving even the clegs.

ROUTE DESCRIPTION

St Catherine's Church Tower

From the layby on the main road near Crook church, a footpath leads diagonally across the field to the wall corner. Continuing above the wall towards the ruined tower, to the right you can see the new church in the valley which was built in 1887. St Catherine's Church Tower, whose fourteenth-century bell was transferred to the new church, sits atop a rocky knoll surrounded by a wall. There are a couple of large ash trees in the churchyard, but only two gravestones, both memorials to members of the Hutchinson family, while inside the shell of the bell tower an iron ladder is tantalisingly just out of reach. Over to the left, the chimneys of Crook Hall can be seen. The house, which dates from around 1620, originally had the unusual name of Twatterden Hall, and was the home of the Royalist, Robert Philipson, who fought against Oliver Cromwell. Both the present hall and the church were built at the beginning of the eighteenth century.

Atkinson Tarn (*Named after its creator*)

Follow the wall along to a squeeze stile and down to a gateway, then turn right on the field track. The track, edged in summer by a wide variety of flowers, follows an old hedgerow, then crosses the field to a gate and bridge over a ditch. Continue beside the wall to join a tarmac lane.

Turning right, the lane leads down across a hay meadow, still as meadows used to be, full of flowers in summer. At the road by Brow Head Farm, where even the steps are whitewashed, turn right down Back Lane to the bridge and then go left on the track. Atkinson Tarn lies just ahead. The secluded sheet of water is a private fishery, surrounded by trees and shrubs, with two wooded islands to encourage nesting birds. This new tarn was created in 1988 by the farmer at Brow Head, and it is already so well established that it is difficult to believe it was made using a waterproof liner in the same way as a garden pond.

Crook (*Bend in the river*)

Follow the walled track along past Spigot House, another beautiful whitewashed residence, then take the footpath which leads across a couple of fields and out to the busy main road by the Howe. Turning right along the road for a short way to Birksey Brow, a kissing gate leads into the fields. The path climbs diagonally to a gate at the top corner, then goes over a step stile and along the wall to pass above Sunnybrow. Across the valley you can see the old church tower, while ahead are the distant soft folds of the Howgills.

At a gap, the path goes down to follow the lower wall along to a wooden step stile. Passing to the left of a barn, the path goes round the back of Boxtree, squeezing through the narrow space behind the house, to a footbridge. The path then keeps below Field Tenement, which has a commanding position overlooking the valley, and though the house is very grand it is still a working farm. Go through a little gate to join the farm track, but leave it at the bend to cross a ladder stile and head for the buildings ahead. A kissing gate leads onto a track by Yew Tree Farm where you turn right and down the farm lane to the new St Catherine's church. The village of Crook is a straggle of houses with no centre and the Sun Inn, the nearest local hostelry, is a good mile away along the busy main road.

ALPHABETICAL LIST OF THE EASTERN TARNS

Name	Grid ref	Walk number
ALCOCK TARN	349079	5.2
ANGLE TARN (Hartsop)	418143	2.5
ARGLES TARN	445870	10.5
ARNSBARROW TARN	311918	9.2
ASH CRAGS TARN	293096	5.1
ATKINSON TARN	447948	11.4
AYSIDE TARN	388839	private
BACK REDDINGS ALLOTMENT	365835	10.3
BARNGATES TARN		see Drunken Duck
BARROW PLANTATION TARN		see Stonehills Tarn
BELL CRAGS TARN	299143	4.1
BIGLAND TARN	355829	10.3
BIGLAND TROUT FISHERY		see Back Reddings
BINSEY HILL TARN	228363	private
BIRKET HOUSES TARN		see Podnet Tarn
BLACK BECK TARN	334871	10.2
BLEA WATER	449108	3.2
BLELHAM FISH POND	363007	dried up
BLELHAM TARN	366006	8.2
BOLTON'S TARN	448935	overgrown
BORETREE TARN	355874	private
BORRANS RESERVOIR	429010	private
BORWICK FOLD TARN	443969	11.1
BOWSCALE TARN	336313	1.2
BRANSTREE TARN	484103	3.3
BROCK CRAGS TARNS	417137	2.5
BROTHERS WATER	402129	2.4
BROWN COVE TARN	344160	2.1
BROWNRIGG MOSS TARN	298104	4.2
BROWNSTONE TARN	383976	8.3
CACER TARN		see Slew Tarn
CANNY HILL TARN	365852	10.3
CARLSIDE TARN	255283	1.4
CASPEL GATE TARN	451113	3.2
CAUDALE MOOR TARN	415101	2.4
CHAPEL HOUSE RESERVOIR	260359	1.1
CLEABARROW TARN	424963	11.1
CODALE HEAD TARNS	288091	5.1

Name	Grid ref	Walk number
CODALE TARN	298088	5.1
CROOK RESERVOIR	445956	private
CUNSWICK TARN	490938	11.3
DAW'S POND	479262	private
DECOY HAG POND	534229	private
DECOY POND (Askham)	532226	private
DOCKEY TARN	353073	dried up
DRUNKEN DUCK TARN	351011	private, by roadside
DUBBS RESERVOIR	422017	6.4
DUCK TARN	404884	private
EASEDALE TARN	308088	5.1
FIDDLER HALL TARN	391855	10.4
FOTHERGILL TARN		see Gurnal Dubbs
FOURSTONES TARN	491164	3.1
GALLS TARN	409004	private
GARNETT BRIDGE TARN		see Routen Beck Tarns
GHYLL HEAD FISH POND	397927	11.2
GHYLL HEAD RESERVOIR	398923	11.2
GHYLL POOL	497985	7.3
GOOSEYFOOT TARN	337970	9.1
GRANGE RESERVOIR		see High Newton
GREAT GREEN HOWS TARN		see Green Howes Upper
GREEN HOWS TARN	362908	private
GREEN HOWS UPPER TARN	360900	private
GREEN TARN	366985	private
GREENHILL TARN		see Jenny Dam
GREENUP EDGE TARNS	288111	4.2
GREYCRAG TARN	491077	overgrown
GRISEDALE TARN	350120	2.2
GRIZEDALE TARN	346945	9.1
GRIZEDALE TARN SMALL	348944	9.1
GUMMER'S HOW TARN	394886	10.4
GURNAL DUBS	502992	7.3
HABER TARN	502224	private
HAGG POND	367983	private
HARD TARN	345138	2.2
HARROP TARN	312136	4.1
HASKEW TARN	521114	3.4
HAYESWATER	430122	2.5
HEIGHTS TARN	401885	private
HELTON TARN	420850	private

Name	Grid ref	Walk number
HIGH ARNSIDE TARN	332012	8.1
HIGH BORRANS RESERVOIR		see Borrans Reservoir
HIGH CROSS TARN		see Wharton Tarn
HIGH DAM	362888	10.1
HIGH MAN TARN	329965	9.1
HIGH MOSS TARN	375980	8.3
HIGH NEWTON RESERVOIRS	400840	private, by roadside
HIGH RIGG TARN	309214	1.3
HIGH TAGGLESHAW	505994	private
HOB GILL TARN		see Wood Moss Tarn
HODSON'S TARN	369982	8.2
HOLEHIRD TARN	409007	6.4
HOLMESHEAD TARN	351024	private, by roadside
HOW TOP TARN	345068	5.2
HOWES TARN	501104	3.3
JACK CROFT POND	524236	private
JENNY DAM	463953	private
JUNIPER TARN	340964	9.1
KEMP TARN	464988	7.4
KENTMERE RESERVOIR	445080	7.5
KENTMERE TARN	453021	7.1
KEPPLECOVE TARN	343166	dried up
KNIPE TARN	427944	11.2
LAMBHOWE TARN	418917	private
LANTY TARN (Howtown)	435190	dried up
LANTY'S TARN (Glenridding)	394164	2.1
LATRIGG TARN	416018	private
LAUNCHY TARN (Thirlmere)	302142	4.1
LILY POND	367984	8.2
LILY TARN	364040	6.1
LINDETH FELL TARN	404952	private
LINDETH TARN	412947	disappeared
LINTHWAITE HOUSE TARN	407954	private
LITTLE LUDDERBURN TARN	403916	overgrown
LITTLE TARN	249338	1.1
LITTLEWATER TARN	509170	private
LODGE HEAD TARN		see Tent Lodge Tarn
LOUGHRIGG FELL TARNS	352047	6.1
LOUGHRIGG TARN	345045	6.1
LOW DAM	364885	10.1
LOW TAGGLESHAW	525992	7.3

Name	Grid ref	Walk number
MIDDLE FAIRBANK TARN	449974	private
MIDDLE TAGGLESHAW	516993	private
MIDDLE TARN	404881	10.4
MIDDLERIGG TARN	398012	6.3
MORTIMERE	364029	private
MOSS ECCLES TARN	372968	8.3
MOSS INTAKE TARN	370991	private
MOSS SIDE TARN	484956	11.3
NEVIN TARN		see Little Tarn
NEWTON TARN	409826	private
NORMOSS TARN	378992	8.2
OUT DUBS TARN	368949	private
OVER WATER	252350	1.1
PLACE FELL TARN	408172	2.3
PODNET TARN	404925	11.2
POTTER TARN	495989	7.3
PRIEST POT	357978	private
RAINSBORROW TARN	443067	7.5
RAISE HOW TARN	339994	private
RATHERHEATH TARN	484958	11.3
RATHERHEATH TARN SMALL	484960	11.3
RAVEN'S BARROW TARN	413876	10.4
RED SCREES TARN	396088	6.2
RED TARN (Helvellyn)	348152	2.1
REDCRAG TARN	450150	3.1
ROBINSON'S TARN	368981	private
ROSE CASTLE TARN	334002	8.1
ROSTHWAITE FARM TARNS	402934	11.2
ROUDSEA TARN	332824	private
ROUGH CRAG TARN		see Steel Fell Tarn
ROUGH HILL TARN	495195	by roadside
ROUTEN BECK - LOW	515911	private
ROUTEN BECK - UPPER	511992	private
ROWANTHWAITE POND	461953	private
SATURA CRAG TARN	423136	2.5
SAWREY STRICELY TARN	338907	private
SCALE HEAD TARN	373975	8.3
SCALE IVY TARN	382962	8.3
SCALE TARN		see Scale Head Tarn
SCALEBARROW TARN	519152	disappeared
SCALES TARN	329281	1.2

Name	Grid ref	Walk number
SCANDALE TARN	386098	6.2
SCHOOL KNOTT TARN	427973	11.1
SCREAM POINT TARN		see Ratherheath Small
SERGEANT MAN TARN	288091	5.1
SIMPSON GROUND RESERVOIR	396864	10.4
SKEGGLES WATER	479035	7.2
SLEW TARN	356030	private
SMALL WATER	453100	3.2
SNIPESHOW TARN	297211	1.3
SOW HOW TARN	401879	10.4
STANDING CRAG TARNS	296137	4.1
STEEL FELL TARN	308112	4.2
STEWART'S RESERVOIR		see Middle Fairbank
STICKS PASS RESERVOIR	357181	disappeared
STONEHILLS TARN	418944	11.2
SUMMERHOUSE POND	368984	private
SWINKLEBANK TARN	503047	no access from valley
TARN HOWS	328999	8.1
TENT LODGE TARN	327972	private
TENTER HOWE TARN	507008	overgrown
TEWET TARN	305236	1.3
THREE DUBS TARN	377974	private
TOBY TARN	443881	10.5
TOM TARN	413818	dried up
TOP DAM		see Sticks Pass Res
UNDERMILLBECK COMMON	424951	private
WATERBARNETS TARN	351011	private, by roadside
WET SLEDDALE RESERVOIR	554115	3.4
WHARTON TARN	331988	8.1
WHITE MOSS TARN (Hay Bridge)	334874	10.2
WHITEMOSS TARN (Rydal)	346068	5.2
WHITESIDE TARN	532010	private, by roadside
WISE EEN TARN	368977	8.3
WITHERSLACK HALL TARN	435864	10.5
WOOD MOSS TARN	328918	9.2
WRAYMIRES TARN	368979	private
WYTHBURN HEAD TARNS	305115	4.2

Printed by
CARNMOR PRINT, LONDON ROAD, PRESTON, U.K.